RICHARD ZENOR "THE INSTRUMENT"

TELEPHONE BETWEEN WORLDS

TELEPHONE BETWEEN WORLDS

BY JAMES CRENSHAW

Foreword by Dr. Gustaf Strömberg

DeVorss Publications

ISBN: 0-87516-692-X
Eleventh Printing, 1996

DeVorss & Company, Publisher
P.O. Box 550
Marina del Rey, CA 90294

Printed in the United States of America

TABLE OF CONTENTS

FOREWORD

By Dr. Gustaf Strömberg*

T HE QUESTION of the possibility of communicating with departed spirits has been the subject of much controversy. Spiritualists claim that they have direct evidence of such communications in the "spirit messages" they have received through mediums. It can not be denied that these messages often involve specific facts known by a particular departed person and by no one else, and that the medium often exhibits an ability which he normally does not possess.

The majority of people, however, regard such messages

* An astronomer of international renown, Dr. Strömberg was a member of the scientific research staff of the Carnegie Institution's Mount Wilson Observatory in California from 1917 to 1946. Besides a large number of papers he has written in his own particular field, he has been a pioneer in the correlation of scientific data pointing to the survival of memory and consciousness after bodily death. This has included the analytical examination of data on certain "living fields" which seem to have their roots in a non-physical world beyond the realm of space and time. His findings and conclusions are contained in two books, THE SOUL OF THE UNIVERSE and THE SEARCHERS (both published by the David McKay Co. of Philadelphia), and have had an important impact upon scientific thinking throughout the world.

as absurd and due either to fraud or to self-deception, and probably of the same nature as dreams and hallucinations, which are generally regarded as manifestations in our consciousness of subconscious mental activities. The primary reason for this attitude is probably a conviction that spiritualistic phenomena violate the laws of nature as recognized by modern science.

There can be no doubt that many alleged spirit messages are the result of activities in the mind of the medium himself, without the cooperation of other minds. Mental activities are to a large extent unpredictable, and the causal relationship involved can not be established. A medium is ordinarily in a kind of sleep, and his conscious reasoning power is lost or greatly reduced. The medium has no means of distinguishing between "voices" originating in his subconscious mind, on the one hand, and those which originate in the minds of other people, on the other hand. It should be obvious that the existence of manufactured, inconsistent or nonsensical messages does not preclude the possibility of a medium expressing ideas of a profound meaning.

During the last fifty years, extensive studies have been made of psychic phenomena, partly by the Societies of Psychical Research and lately by universities of high standing in the United States and Europe. A mass of evidence has been collected which, among other things, has proved that the phenomena of telepathy and clairvoyance are certainly real and involve a direct communication between the minds of different people. The reason why the reality of such phenomena has not been generally accepted lies—and this is an interesting commentary on the way of thinking in the modern world—not in any inconsistency or incompleteness in the evidence itself, but in the absence of any scientific theory which could account for the observed facts. The same applies in an even higher degree to the reason for the general disbelief in spirit messages, particularly since the evidence here is less convincing.

In recent years some progress has been made in the development of scientific theories for the explanation of psychic phenomena in general. One of these theories was developed, not to explain psychic phenomena, but to give a satisfactory explanation of the high degree of organization in the living world and of the relationship between our nervous system and our mental activities.

The basic assumption made was that the fields of force, which govern the motions and the configurations of particles and atoms in inorganic as well as in organic matter, represent our way of picturing energy patterns of complex structure which themselves were regarded as the physical manifestations of activities of another type. According to this theory, our nerve cells, nerve systems and brains have properties somewhat similar to our radio receiving sets. They are of cosmic origin, and through them we can establish a direct communication with pre-existing mental qualities in a non-physical world. Our nerve cells have their "roots" and their origin in a world transcending that of the physical world of space and time, and they make it possible for us to become aware of colors and sounds, of feelings and emotions, of will and ideas, and to remember past events. These and similar mental qualities all belong to a non-physical world, and when our nerve cells are stimulated by one means or another, we become consciously aware of their existence.

In the living world are organizing fields which determine the structure and functions of all living organisms and their organs. These fields are well defined. They expand during embryonic development, reach their full size at maturity, and at death they contract to a point and disappear into the non-physical world from which they originally came. All our memories are "engraved" in our brain field, which has a definite electrical structure with the aid of which it determines and stabilizes the structure and functions of our brains. When at death our "memory field" contracts and disappears from the physical world, it retains all its mental elements in unchanged form. In this way we can obtain a scientific picture of the phenomena of life and death, and we even arrive at a theory for the survival of the soul with a retention of all its memories.

(Many of the electrical manifestations of these so-called living fields have recently been studied at the Medical School of Yale University. A description of the theory and references to the scientific literature are given in the second edition of my book, THE SOUL OF THE UNIVERSE. The new ideas are described in another form in my new book, THE SEARCHERS, where the problem of the immortality of the human soul has been analyzed in an Epilogue.)

It is clear that if souls survive at death without any loss of memory and if our mind is able to communicate with a non-physical world in which it is rooted, it should, at least in principle, be possible to contact the minds of departed persons. The theory indicates that the mechanism involved consists in a stimulation of specific nerve centers, which we all probably possess, although they may be little developed among most people and highly developed among others. Since we can expect that the "intensity" of the stimulation is of great importance, specific abilities of the person "on the other side" should play an important role in the establishment of communication.

As described in the present book by James Crenshaw, the teachings of Agasha, the master who we are told speaks through the mouth of Richard Zenor, are on a very high ethical level. Agasha is stated to be a very wise man who lived some 7000 years ago, and his philosophy compares favorably with those of the great thinkers of the world. It is inconceivable that Richard Zenor, who never had any opportunity to study philosophy, could of himself construct, consciously or subconsciously, the system of thought he describes. There are also statements of other types which certainly can not be ascribed to a knowledge possessed by Richard Zenor himself.

James Crenshaw is a well known and conscientious reporter, and he describes facts as he sees or hears them. For this reason I am convinced that the present book will prove of interest to many people and will contribute to our knowledge of a field of inquiry which has just begun to be explored.

Pasadena, California, August, 1948

Gustaf Strömberg

INTRODUCTION

I<small>T</small> <small>USED TO BE</small> socially unacceptable for one to display a marked or serious interest in psychic phenomena or the theory of communication between this and the after-life world. Fortunately, such an interest now is widely regarded as almost respectable, and we find men and women of science, of letters and in other positions of high standing espousing the tenets of communication quite openly, without much fear of the vicious reprisals that dogged the careers of pioneers like Crookes, Lodge and Conan Doyle.

Now we have universities which offer courses in psychic research. We have serious laboratory investigations of spirit phenomena. We have dozens of learned societies which carry on widespread and thoroughgoing researches, and we have, both in the New and the Old World, millions of persons who claim to have found a satisfying religious philosophy in the principles and `teachings expressed through inter-world communication.

So much, therefore, has gone before to lay the founda-tions for the present short work that an outline of its lim-ited scope and purpose is advisable. In the first place, it is not to be considered in any way a general treatment of psychic phenomena or mediumship, but merely an abridged report of the nature of one kind of mediumship and the results which that has achieved. Second, it is not a compendium of psychic evidence. The student can easily find thousands of books, reports and articles overflowing with the proofs of communication without relying upon the few examples in these pages. Third, there is no presumption herein to convert the reader to a new philosophy, because the fact is that there is nothing new in what has been set down—only a simple restatement of what is immeasurably old and eternal.

Other than to attempt an interesting and helpful source of information with a fresh viewpoint on an old subject, the present endeavor is calculated to inspire, if possible, an inclination on the part of the reader to search within his own consciousness for those ultimate answers which, after all, must be finally supplied by one's self. No attempt has been made to give all the answers here, because that would be impossible anyway. The limitations of language alone would preclude even a misguided attempt to do so, assuming all the answers were known. The search and the journey must always be lonely, each choosing a path appropriate to his development and encountering now and then a sign post that indicates the True Way. If in the capacity of a reporter I have erected a guide post or two for some, I am sure I shall have fulfilled in part my reason for being.

During most of my life I have been a reporter, and the reportorial instinct for accuracy, terseness and simplicity, I hope, has not now become submerged. I realize, of course, the danger of over-simplification, and I know that many things have been left unsaid that should probably have been said for greater clarity. Many other things have been said which are only clumsy approximations of the truth and could have been better said. But I have attempted to give as much direct information as possible and as little interpretation as is consistent with a coherent presentation. It is merely well to remember how precarious is the task of the writer who boldly sets about to put down in words that which really is beyond words—despite a judicious condensation and distillation of the expressions in the vernacular which have been furnished by the Teachers of Wisdom. Words are by their very nature the related and ambiguous symbols of our local illusions, rather than universal expressions of illimitable reality. Yet now and again they touch a button which closes a circuit that illuminates the neophyte with a flood of understanding from the limitless Source of illumination already present within him.

Once we accept the fact that authoritative information can come to us from sources beyond our earthly ken—beyond the realm of ordinary laboratory proofs and empirical methods—we have gone far toward establishing a permanent pathway for our understanding. We are prone to proceed in our living as though a certain truth does not exist until it has been established by our crude and limited methods of observation, whereas many things are undoubtedly true which vitally affect our lives, even though we have no inkling of them. A military commander who assumed that no new tactic or mechanism of war need be considered other than those listed in his textbooks would certainly court disaster. We need not be gullible to assume *a priori* principles not necessarily demonstrable at the moment, nor does such an attitude preclude the constant testing of such purported truths as are susceptible to our analysis. But where we have some reason to believe that sources of information are available to us from inter-stellar space, so to speak, it behooves us to examine the information as hypothetically reasonable and to apply it to our current understanding for the purpose of stimulating our expanding realization from within. We need not probe blindly, then, but connectively and less speculatively, following the lighted path of those wise souls who believe we should not be left floundering in a kindergarten of confusion without guidance and with only our simple, local environment on which to base our conclusions.

The teachers who speak through Richard Zenor have constantly emphasized that we all, in reality, are infinitely intelligent and that our continuing experience, combined with the realization we may achieve through the prompting of those who have already grown into wisdom, insures the gradual expression of boundless intelligence. The Way can be made pleasant and joyful if we listen well to the counsel of those who have preceded us.

This is the age, say the teachers, when even the profounder aspects of science and religion—of revelation, if you please—will be resolved into a single system without serious conflict. We begin to see a glimmer of reality in this promise when, for instance, we first hear such a one as Agasha say that, in the realm of the totality he calls the "Universal Consciousness," one can be "here, there and everywhere" simultaneously, that everything is a part of the All and the All is within everything. And then we hear a popular exposition of Einstein's findings, with references to the interrelatedness of space and the relative nature of the time concept as inherent in the properties of space. Does there not seem to be a connection?

Are not our philosophical and scientific concepts becoming more nearly true as our philosophy becomes less speculative and more authoritative? We are privileged to improvise our tests and search for our proofs to our hearts' content, but our puny methods of resolving singularly local doubts must seem ridiculous in the sight of the ageless wise ones whose axioms partake of immutable principles that support all the worlds, whether we choose to believe them or not. In our meager kindergarten, it may be well for us to listen and try to understand that which they have accepted, observed and understood for eons, rather than to scrabble obstinately in the comfortless anarchy of our conceits.

I have studied, observed and investigated the telephone-like instrumentality of Richard Zenor for more than a dozen years. For one full year, I lived in his home and grew to know his personality, as distinct from the personalities that manifest through his mediumship, as well as almost anyone else I know.

There were many evidences, both subtle and directly apparent, of the authenticity of his mediumship, but over the years, the conviction has grown that it is not merely the remarkable indications of the simple truth of communication with another world that are important about Richard Zenor's work. Rather, I have become impressed with the profound, though often simply stated, insight into basic meanings which are given by the higher teachers through his instrumentality. Knowing him as I do, knowing his personality, his capacities and limitation, watching the changing and distinctive expressions of his face and his bodily movements when others are controlling him and then dimly realizing the deep significance of the teachings which have been brought through him, I have become certain that the ordinary tools and methods of psychic research are entirely inadequate to present a fair picture of his mediumship. Too often we forget that there are more things in heaven and earth than are dreamed of in our laboratories.

While I have striven, therefore, to give in condensed form a scribe's "fair report" of the communications which this remarkable instrument presents, I have sought principally to set down words which by their very context may well establish the verity of the phenomena and lend credence to the claim of authority. Once that authority is accepted, the restatement of changeless truths becomes as a beacon in space, bidding us look upward and outward beyond the restrictive confines of our mortal coil into the hidden meanings of the universe behind the universe. No other kind of instrument, no giant telescope, no fabulously equipped laboratory can perform the cosmic function so well.

The reader will bear in mind, if he please, that neither I nor Richard Zenor, nor the teachers, including Agasha himself, is any one of us the ultimate source of what little of approximate truth is set forth. Rather, each of us, including the reader, is the true source, to the extent, as we have tried to emphasize, that the words take on individual meanings which are awakening expressions of our own infinite intelligence. We all are intermediaries, filtering that which has its origin in the universal source of wisdom down to the level of our present state of understanding. Some who are farther along on the path of unfoldment speak with greater authority because they are less inhibited by the environment of their illusions, but finally what every one of us is trying to express is the true and good in all the great religions and philosophies of the past and the future, because we find that the differences become important only as they obscure the similarities. Truth has many facets, but the Jewel in the Lotus is always the same.

THE INSTRUMENT

I

DURING HIS LIFETIME, it is now well known that Thomas A. Edison considered and experimented with the possibility of communicating between the material world and the so-called after-life world by means of a mechanism he hoped to perfect.

This "telephone between worlds" would have operated on the assumption that the difference between the world we are now in and the world of the hereafter is one of degree rather than kind; that is, the natural laws which prevail here are of such universal character that they prevail also in the "hereafter." The rules thus are the same. Only the emphasis changes.

Therefore, the idea of developing a method of communication between intelligences in different *degrees* of consciousness has seemed to many profound thinkers to be no more implausible than communication between persons in different *places* of consciousness.

The fact is that such instruments of communication—between the world of this life and the life beyond—have been available in many lands throughout the ages. They have operated with varying degrees of efficiency and in a variety of forms, ranging from symbols and signals to the spoken word. But the mechanism up to the present has always been the human body itself.

Many believe—and there have been a large number of experiments to support the contention—that everyone possesses to a greater or lesser degree what are known as "psychic" powers. In most, these psychic faculties are submerged and undeveloped. In others, they are capable of development. But in a very few, such faculties are evident almost from birth. There is something in their bodily chemistry and their mental makeup which appears to cause them to be extraordinarily sensitive to what are commonly known as "psychic vibrations."

The Rev. Richard Zenor, of the Agasha Temple of Wisdom in Los Angeles, is such a "sensitive" or medium. He is in truth an "instrument" by means of which we are able to carry on direct communication between worlds almost as easily as if we were connected by telephone.

How it is that he happens to have this gift we cannot say, any more than we can explain with certainty why a musical prodigy can play a particularly difficult concerto before the age of five or another young genius can understand the principles of the differential and integral calculus before the age of ten. All we can be sure of is that these gifts sometimes become manifest at a very early age, while to develop anything like them in ordinary individuals may require the greater part of a lifetime, assuming they can be developed at all.

Richard Zenor has been known for his unusual psychic faculties since he was four years old. It was then that he told his mother of visions and of "visitors" whom others could not see. A less understanding mother might have dismissed it all as "imagination" or even have punished him for telling untruths. (There have been such cases— children beaten for insisting upon the presence of invisible playmates, or scolded and left bewildered because others claimed to be unaware of scenes so clear to the honest child.)

In school, he says he would somehow know the right answers in an examination without studying. At other times, correct replies to verbal questions would flash into his mind instantaneously. He came to be regarded as different from other children, particularly so when, later on, he would fall into a kind of coma or trance without explanation. This caused considerable alarm when it occurred at his school in Terre Haute, Ind., but again his mother was well enough acquainted with these matters to recognize, not the symptoms of a psychosis, but of a psychic.

She finally took him to a mediumistic circle, and she tells of how his own abilities as a trumpet and direct voice medium were immediately discovered. From that time forward, it was difficult to turn away the scores of friends, neighbors and others interested in his new found powers. During this period, she says he gave demonstrations from time to time, not only of this well known form of communication, but other phenomenal phases as well, including materialization, levitation and apportation. At home, a phonograph would wind itself and play records seemingly without human aid. Sometimes objects or the child himself would be lifted and carried in midair, a phenomenon which often occurred unexpectedly and on occasions when the person most startled and impressed was Richard himself.

His family never quite got used to these things, much as they tried to understand them. His sister once was astonished to find before her the full-form materialization of a close friend, completely life-like, despite the fact that he had "died" a short time before.

The life of Richard's father was once saved in Colorado by a heeded warning from the boy who saw visions. In this latter case, Richard repeatedly had a vision of an explosion at a mine in which his father owned an interest. Finally, the mental picture became so vivid on a particular day that his mother was impressed with the boy's agitation and prevailed upon her husband not to enter the mine. He was thus saved, but a number of workmen were killed in the accident Richard had seen in advance so clearly; that is, "clairvoyantly."

Another incident serves to illustrate the extra-sensory faculties which he began to manifest while very young: He had been put to bed for an afternoon nap, and he slept soundly, but after he had awakened he told his mother with naive candor that he had "gone out of the window" from the bedroom and had taken his dog with him into town (five miles away) to be with his father. He then reported in detail his father's activities.

At dinner time, Richard's father started to give his own report of the day's happenings, but he was interrupted by his wife's declaration that she already knew what he had been doing. To prove it, she told him—in the same detail given to her earlier by the young boy. The father was naturally astonished, but then admitted he had found the dog in town and, after transacting certain business, had brought the animal home with him. He did not see his son, of course, for—as occultists would say—the boy was having an "astral flight." His invisible astral body and ego had left his physical outer-shell during sleep and had traveled with the dog to see his father. This experience was the precursor of Richard's later ability to leave his body voluntarily, thereby making it available for use as a "telephone."

Meantime, those outside his family marveled and wondered at equally remarkable experiences. Richard began to be known as the "Wonder Boy"—wonderful because he had powers which others seemed not to have and which they could not explain. The story is even told of how he helped to locate a cache of treasure. A Chinese had buried approximately $10,000 in cash not far from where Richard was then living in Colorado. Like many another mortal, the Oriental found that he could not take it with him when he departed from the earthly life. So when a friend of the dead man visited the boy (who had by now developed as a trumpet medium), a message came through from the Oriental in characteristic language: The money would be found at such-and-such a spot. It was, but Richard says the finder never was grateful enough to offer to share any part of the small fortune he had located.

Among the many letters which Richard received, acknowledging his unusual abilities, is a typical one from a friend in Topeka, Kansas. Dated March 24, 1927, it read:

"Dear Richard—,

"Want to say that I located my nephew through your direction. I think it was wonderful on your part. He lives in a large two (2) story house as you pictured to me.

"I rec'd a letter from [name of mutual friend] & she gave me your address. I wanted to drop you a line & thank you for the information you gave me. Hope I can be lots of help to you sometime. . . ."

Up to this point, Richard Zenor's history is very similar to that of scores of other youngsters who have attracted attention because of psychic gifts. At about the age of twelve, however, Richard began a new and rarer phase of mediumship. The change happened suddenly with no other warning than the boy's own statement that he felt something different was about to happen to him. It did that night. Instead of speaking through a trumpet, voices began coming through his own lips, but only after he had lapsed into the now familiar trance.

He himself had literally become a telephone link between two worlds, the instrument whereby those no longer clothed in the physical garment, as we know it, could speak naturally and directly to those left behind.

This new phase, replacing as it did his other phenomena, was in a sense a disappointment to the boy medium. Before, it had been possible for him to be conscious of what was going on around him during his demonstrations. He could hear the messages himself and enjoy the other manifestations which he, as well as others, found so entertaining and informative. Now, however, he was entirely unconscious (at least, he said he remembered nothing when he awoke) during all the time his body was being used as an instrument of communication.

Nevertheless, the voices which henceforth were heard through him, often exhibiting personality traits much too mature and adult for a young boy, attracted thousands to his demonstrations, and it became more and more apparent that this must be his life work. Scientists puzzled over the foreign tongues that were spoken from his lips; medical men made tests to see if they could determine what was different about him, and psychic research societies conducted their investigations. Most all agreed on one thing: Richard was not abnormal, but his manifestations were certainly supernormal.

When he was 18, he was accompanied on a tour by a medical doctor who studied his every movement and reaction. I have copied the essential parts of a letter which this physician wrote in Portland, Ore., on December 18, 1930, and reproduce them here:

"My dear Richard:

"As our trip is about to close and we will, for awhile, at least, separate, I want to express to you some of the thoughts and convictions that I have experienced, while with you.

"Altho feeling that a future life was essential to make the life on Earth reasonable and just, I have not been able for many years to believe in future existence. Most doctors share with me this conviction. But after being with you, and witnessing the demonstrations through your mediumship, I have no other alternative but to be convinced, intellectually, that we do go on living after we pass thru Death. . . .

"I believe in you and your demonstrations, and know that with the proper background and management, you will become known nationally in a few years. While being sorry I cannot at the present time go on with you, the time may come that at some future date we may be together.

"This appreciation is shared with the vast majority of those with whom we have come in contact, and I know that in every town you have left behind many sincere friends and converts to Spiritualism. . . .

No one who saw Richard Zenor's demonstrations could fail in some way to be impressed, not because they were theatrically sensational (they were not), but because the very naturalness and ingenuousness of the phenomena could appeal to thinkers and searchers. Others of little mind, looking only for the spectacular, or the ignorantly prejudiced, totally immersed in their own preconceptions, might dismiss the whole business with the overworked cry of "fraud," but any who reflected soon concluded that this answer was less than inadequate to meet the questions which must arise.

I confess to a considerable measure of skepticism when I first encountered Richard Zenor. It was during a week of demonstrations before standing-room-only audiences in a Los Angeles Protestant church, where he was the guest of the regular "orthodox" minister. I remember that a relatively unimportant matter first gave me a subtle inkling that there was something different about this youth: Voices which spoke from his own lips and used his vocal cords often referred to him objectively as "the boy"—"the boy's face," "the boy's hands," "the boy's voice" and similar expressions.

My curiosity aroused, the unanswered and seemingly unanswerable questions which emerged caused me to arrange a demonstration for a special committee, including a professor of philosophy at a Los Angeles university. Due to a bizarre twist of circumstance, the tests ended on a rather sad and sour note. I had taken along a photographer to make pictures of the committee and the subject of their examination. It was suggested that he might also try for "spirit" photos, although there was no claim that Mr. Zenor possessed this specialized phase of mediumship.

However, the photographer later reported that he had obtained a clear "extra" of a little Chinese girl on one of the photographs of the group. (A female child's voice had spoken and sung in Chinese through the medium during one of the manifestations.) I soon determined that the "extra" had been lifted from a current magazine and added to the group photo by a simple trick of photographic makeup, but I was more chagrined to learn a short time afterward that the photographer had convinced Mr. Zenor that the fake picture was authentic and had made arrangements to sell him a number of prints at a very handsome price. Fortunately, I was able to quash the deal. I decided, however, that such naivete certainly tended to prove the hypothesis that Richard Zenor as a person—in this instance, an obviously inexperienced and gullible person—could not conceivably be responsible for the wide range of communications or the profound philosophical content of the lectures which came from his physical mechanism during self-induced sleep. Some other hypothesis than fraud would have to be discovered.

Up to this writing, my observations have covered approximately a dozen years, including one full year that I lived in the same home with Mr. Zenor. Sometimes patiently, other times impatiently, I have tried during the years to collect the material which would, at least in part, explain rationally what others so easily dismiss irrationally, sometimes after witnessing perhaps only a single demonstration. In the following chapters, some of the resultant findings are presented as a kind of outline and introduction for anyone who cares to scan further the broad vistas of potential enlightenment. Each must seek his own answers, and the elusive Total Answer will always be over the horizon. Yet one becomes increasingly aware that the search for it must become the most important concern of our existence.

The way can be opened through such a one as Richard Zenor; but it must be remembered that all channels are not clear channels, and of those channels which do afford a relatively undistorted glimpse of the Source of Wisdom, there will ever be physical limitations which must be divorced from any correct evaluation of the content of their offerings. The limitations may affect and modify the quality of that which is offered, but its value as wisdom must be gauged according to universal, rather than personal, terms.

I have seen Richard Zenor beset by the same kind of vicissitudes and foibles that harry us all; his humanness as a personality is not lost because he is a "telephone." The fine results of his instrumentality, I have concluded, however, are above and apart from the manifestations of his personality. They can and do affect each other, but their separateness is no longer deniable. The manner in which Mr. Zenor met and married the former Thelma Turner is an example in point. Their romance began long after I had become acquainted with him. In fact, I knew him first, so I am able to verify some of the facts from personal knowledge.

Mrs. Turner, a telephone company supervisor at the time, was grieving over the death of her first husband when, approximately six months after his decease, she was induced by a friend to try the "telephone between worlds." It worked well. Her husband identified himself in a number of ways—by mentioning their plans for the last Christmas holidays, which had been interrupted by his hospitalization; by mentioning a string of costume pearls which she had purchased despite a friendly controversy during his lifetime over the value of such "junk" ("I see you got the beads," he remarked jocularly through the medium), and by referring to incidents which occurred during his illness when, as he now explained, he was attempting to conceal from her the fact that he knew he could not survive.

He also asked a significant question: "How did the case come out?" Mrs. Zenor explains that just before his death his mother had been the loser in a legal suit in Texas, but the news was concealed from her son for fear of upsetting him. He was told the outcome of the case months later via the inter-world "telephone."

The young widow had vowed she would never remarry, but through her attendance in the Zenor classes, a friendship developed which finally changed her mind. As Mrs. Zenor, however, I have observed that she is still an eager, questioning, learning student, who regards her husband's instrumentality as entirely separate from his easy-going, good-humored, every-day self.

Her first husband talked less and less of her material problems as time went on, she says, and more of his advancement in the other world. After she began to plan her marriage, she tells of how he expressed his attitude—unthinkable in a material world, but logical for him.

"I'm satisfied," she quotes him as saying through the instrument. "Now that you're taken care of, I can go on."

This was one final bit of identifying evidence, for he had always managed their business affairs almost without consulting her—he had considered her, a woman, incapable of handling them properly—so he had been concerned about how she would fare in the event she were left alone.

One more small incident may illustrate the objectivity with which Richard Zenor himself regards his own work. In the fall of 1943, a brush fire threatened his home in the Woodland Hills section of Los Angeles. He and Mrs. Zenor fought it with a garden hose—and at the same time engaged in an excited metaphysical discussion of free will and destiny. Why, he wanted to know, couldn't the master teachers—who promised help to so many—protect their home? Or was it their karma to have their home destroyed? (The latter was Mrs. Zenor's breathless suggestion.) The home was saved, but the experience points up the truism that, despite the wise words so often uttered through him, Richard Zenor, the personality distinct from the instrument, must be subject to many of the same philosophical errors and misapprehensions that beguile the rest of us.

It is notable that the entities who do the communicating through Richard Zenor continue to refer to him as their "instrument." He is—rather, his body is—a very specialized kind of instrument, a telephone that reproduces speech with the utmost naturalness under ideal conditions but is subject to the limitations of any instrument which requires skill and aptitude for successful manipulation.

Those best qualified to describe how this instrument works should be the persons in the other world from whom communications are received. Here is what they say:

When the medium goes into a deep trance, a kind of displacement occurs which is similar to the change at death, except that a connection is maintained between the displaced spiritual or astral body and the physical body. The spirit of Richard Zenor, with its central soul, its ego and astral body (an exact replica of the physical), actually steps out of the physical shell, whose parts and organs continue to function in a quasi-normal manner. Assisting entities—particularly a "doorkeeper" who has taken the name "Dr. Navajo"—protect it from unwanted intruders.

The process has been described thus by one of the communicators:

"The way the many friends control the instrument's body, principally those who come regularly, is what we might term 'soul projection.' Now, I use that term because we must project ourselves and control the nervic center; automatically we think, and that thought produces the sound, just like you do in your own physical body. But the medium's spirit must step aside and go into the astral consciousness, to remain there until we have finished bringing forth our messages. Some people call it a certain kind of hypnosis. We do not choose to use that word; yet we know we have full power and possession of his body.

"Any great or sudden shock to his physical body or any great disturbance would naturally be felt in the solar plexus of the medium. We try to protect his body so nothing can hurt him and try to use his body with the greatest of care.

"We know, then, that it is necessary on this side of life to have a doorkeeper who is attuned to the medium's body and who permits your loved ones to control. If they are new, they are not going to know just how to control; so the manipulation of the physical body itself will have to come from the doorkeeper."

Anyone watching Richard Zenor change from his role of a normal human being to that of an instrument for communication would see nothing very spectacular. He seats himself relaxedly in a chair, closes his eyes, concentrates for a few moments and then appears to fall into a deep sleep. This is all, except that physicians have observed that his pulse and heartbeat stop for a second or two at the moment of the changeover, and a few other physiological changes have likewise been noted.

The shell is now in a position to be animated by a new and independent entity. This is possible, we are told, only because the medium has certain bodily characteristics which enable another spirit to possess or control the vacated shell without damage to it or its normal occupant. He, in turn, we are told, is fully conscious of the etheric or spirit world while he is out of the body-shell but preserves no memory of his activities there after he emerges from the trance state.

At all times the connection between the spiritual body and the physical is maintained through what is called the "silver cord," an etheric appendage with mysterious properties and the possibility of apparent unlimited extension. When the cord is broken, due to shock, disease or accident, death of the physical form ensues.

The separation of the composite spiritual form from the earth body is possible in all individuals before death, and has been noted by many occultists who use such terms as "astral flights" and "soul projection." There are also numerous recorded instances of persons who have reported seeing their own physical bodies during operations, illnesses or while under the influence of drugs. Occasionally an individual is pronounced "dead," only to be revived later. He may then tell how, from a point in mid-air, he could view all that went on around his body without being able to move or talk; or often he will describe scenes of unearthly beauty. No doubt these last would have been encountered during an artificially induced astral flight, according to the general theory of the disassociation and animation of body by spirit.

A trance medium, however, has a body whose peculiar chemistry and composition enable many, though not all, discarnate entities—that is, persons who have been separated from their own physical bodies—to animate his physical shell whenever he intentionally vacates it. Stepping into the shell, the spirit visitor is able to animate the vacant body, perhaps a little more clumsily, but still much in the same way as the absent owner. In some instances, the visitor finds he can walk around the room, can move arms, hands and head in a natural fashion and, above all, if he has to any extent mastered the control of the vocal cords, he can talk.

Moreover, by the manner of his speech, the use of characteristic gestures and by the subtle mannerisms which are a combination of both of these, the visiting entity can make his own individual personality evident. Most striking examples of personality survival are seen when the manifesting spirit is of foreign origin. Besides speaking in his native language or with an accent, a Chinese, as an example, will accompany his speaking with typical bowing and gesturing, easily recognizable as authentic by anyone familiar with these mannerisms. Equally authentic are the gestures and manner of speaking of, say, a Tibetan priest, a Hindu mystic, an American Indian or a Russian soldier, to say nothing of the many other personalities of the kind one encounters in every day life.

In a particular instance, a lady experienced no difficulty in identifying her husband by means of his gestures alone. During his earthly lifetime, he had been afflicted with an ailment which caused him to move his arms and hands in a nervous, fluttering manner, entirely unlike anyone else. Not sufficiently advanced to overcome this tendency upon returning temporarily to the earthly environment, the same gestures were reproduced through the medium's body. (Neither person had previously been known to Richard Zenor.)

While some personality traits characteristic of the individual who has gone on are generally noted, these depend upon a complexity of factors, ranging from the power (sometimes called "vibrational strength") of the spirit communicator to the receptiveness of the person or persons receiving the communication. The individual in spirit, it must be remembered, is functioning—veritably floating—in a quivering field of force which closely governs all his reactions and is highly susceptible to outside interference.

For example, a person in the physical body whose thoughts are hostile or even tensely nervous can easily produce a mental atmosphere which will have a profound effect on or even block the entity struggling to express itself through a body it has never before used. A receptive attitude, neither too eager nor too restrained, calmly relaxed and conversational, will produce a vibrational environment best suited to the needs of the communicator. And it is axiomatic that a harmonious, untroubled frame of mind on the part of the one seeking the communication, devoid of antagonisms and emotional tensions, will produce the least static and interference for the entity trying desperately to project itself through the quivering sea of vibration. Conversely, the communicator's "power" can be built up and sustained through the help of the person on this end of the line. By "broadcasting" harmonious thoughts, welcoming the visitor, the power for communication is bolstered just as surely as a sympathetic audience creates a stimulating atmosphere for an actor or actress.

Of course, there are those on the "other side" with sufficient experience and a battery of power achieved through advancement in the spiritual realms who practically never encounter great difficulty in controlling the instrument.

Yet we must remember that even these are bound to react to vibrational hazards and suffer certain personality modifications, if for no other reason than that they have to use a strange set of vocal cords, tuned to the voice pattern of a particular individual, namely, Richard Zenor, and temporarily inhabit a body whose own basic vibrational pattern, creating as it does its own strongly personalized mental environment, must necessarily affect their own.

These limitations when clearly understood bring about a fuller appreciation of the conspicuous achievements of the "instrument." For example, women's voices, because of the physical limitations of the voice box, will all tend to sound about the same, as is also true of children's voices. Nevertheless, they will appear to be true feminine and true children's voices, rather than mere mimicry, and personality changes will be observed in the mode of expression of each speaker including facial expressions and bodily movements. Men's voices permit a greater latitude of expression, though still exhibiting the same basic quality of sound production restricted to the capabilities of the body which is being momentarily borrowed.

Yet, with all the vagaries of the mental world as it contacts the physical, the "telephone between worlds" more often than not produces astonishing results which are both satisfying and instructive. The novice has but to remember that the person who is trying to talk to him through this instrument is as anxious as he to complete the transmission. The novelty of the operation and the general excitement of the occasion are not alone confined to the receiver. In all likelihood, the spirit personality is experiencing problems in control as difficult as those of a beginner trying to drive an automobile or ride a bicycle. The effort, successful or otherwise, is deserving of sympathy and cooperation, as well as a minimum of jarring disturbance in the mental atmosphere.

More specifically, these pointers for ideal communication are urged:

(1) Preserve a relaxed, receptive attitude, uncomplicated by thoughts either hostile or confusing. Antagonism will invariably repel the communicator.

(2) Reply promptly and naturally when addressed by someone speaking through the instrument.

(3) If the transmitting entity has trouble controlling the medium, keep talking without excitement or insistence. Recognition of the visitor often builds up confidence and strength.

(4) Carry on a normal conversation with the speaker, avoiding sudden or sharp changes in subject matter which will, so to speak, "rock the boat" by producing a cross-wind in the mental atmosphere.

(5) Avoid unusual or exaggerated emotional demonstrations. These can upset and confuse the visiting spirit as much or more than an attitude of belligerence or antagonism.

(6) Above all, be cheerful and make the visitor welcome.

(7) Remember that evidentiary or test material is more likely to occur spontaneously and unexpectedly than by plan. It is, of course, quite permissible to seek verification of identity by asking leading questions, but this should be done cleverly and carefully so as not to produce the kind of "cross-wind" which might upset the delicate balance of the relationship between spirit and body.

For example, instead of demanding bluntly, "What was Aunt Susie's maiden name?" or, "If you're really Uncle Buckingham, tell me, where did you hide the family jewels?" One might say, "Have you seen any of Aunt Susie's family lately?" or, "Oh, I'm so happy to talk to you, Uncle Buck; I've been searching for something, and I thought perhaps you could help."

Probably in the first instance the speaker will name with enthusiasm any number of Aunt Susie's relatives, and in the case of Uncle Buckingham, will promptly volunteer full information as to the lost jewels, provided he wants them found and knows where they are. (Much stranger things have actually happened—valuable legal papers have been found, lost rings located and missing parts of a chemical formula supplied.)

The success of the test—a fact which even some experts seem unable to understand—depends upon the ability of the questioner to direct the visiting spirit's attention to a subject without requiring him or her to change his whole mental focus suddenly at a time when it is necessary to concentrate on the tricky business of controlling the speaking mechanism of the instrument. The process of question and answer through this type of instrument may be likened to a tightrope walker being cross-examined in the midst of his act. An expert with experience will likely come off better, but an amateur may sometimes do well too. In either case, a good deal of concentration is required and the results will depend upon a natural or acquired ability to maintain balance and control.

Again it should be fully understood that the best "tests" in a large majority of cases are unplanned and unexpected, such as the unexpected use of a word or phrase peculiar to the spirit speaker; the special gesture which marked his personality; the casual mention of a name, place, incident or object of which only he could know the details.

Furthermore, do not decide that the whole subject of

communication is suspect simply because the test you had hoped for was not as you had expected or was not exactly to your liking. Your experience will neither totally prove nor disprove the theory of communication—only add to the mountains of evidence already accumulated in such vast amounts that only old-fashioned mossback materialists and ignorantly closed minds any longer categorically disbelieve.

Reasonableness is advised at all times, if results are desired. No telephone will produce a communication beyond the capabilities of the communicators, and the conversation depends as much upon the personality, intelligence and state of mind of the receiver as of the transmitter. As an example of unreasonableness, there was an occasion when an incredulous gentleman suddenly addressed the medium in French, having heard that personalities speaking French had in the past come through the instrument. Since the spirit in control of the medium at the moment had no knowledge of French and was completely confused as to the purpose of this outburst, the purported "test" was a complete failure.

The unexpected and unsolicited "test" is in many ways the most satisfying, because its spontaneity does much to remove the natural tendency toward doubt. Also, the spontaneous test often is built around some reference or allusion quite remote from the mind of the person receiving the communication. This tends to eliminate the "scientific" skeptic's second line of defense, namely, that it is all a kind of mind reading or telepathy—this in spite of the fact that the same person most likely would resist any theory of telepathy on its own ground with equal vigor.

One is bound to be somewhat impressed, however,

when a distinctly feminine voice speaks through Richard Zenor's lips and says quite unexpectedly, "Oh, I see you're still wearing the blue dress I gave you!" The person wearing the blue dress having for the time being forgotten about the gift, she was, of course, thrilled by this evidential statement.

Names which hold a significance for the person communicating and the one receiving likewise flow into the conversations in a natural way, much like long distance telephone greetings on the physical plane. Following is an example of the kind of unprompted reference to names which is less the exception than the rule through the inter-world "telephone":

VOICE (through medium, after announcing itself as "Dad") : Sadie is here. Sally is here. Elizabeth is here. In fact, they are all here, but they can't all talk to you. They don't have the time. They are all here, anyhow.

Conversely, it has been my observation that, where the prospective "receiver" is obviously antagonistic or hostile or has a "show-me-or-else" attitude, the communications have a tendency to be choked, garbled or, if successful in any manner, gasped out with the difficulty of a great struggle.

Not all of the convincing proofs of the workability of the "instrument" are in the form of communications which identify the communicator. Occasionally, the speaking entity will tell of his or her activities away from the instrument, relating events and observations which could not have been easily reported by anyone not there. The little girl, Marjorie, who for many years has been one of the regular band of "controls" for the medium, once left a Zenor class meeting and returned to describe accurately the appearance of a new cat which had joined the household of one of the class members.

Another time I asked Marjorie to go to my home and report back what was happening there. She returned a few minutes later, saying that "everything's under control" and that Mrs. Crenshaw was "writing to beat the band." (She actually was using the typewriter, although I did not know it at the time.) Following is the remainder of the conversation:

MARJORIE: Does she make some kind of drink for you when you get home?

J.C.: Not that I know of. Why?

MARJORIE: Because she was making some kind of drink, and she had cups out.

J.C.: Maybe she was making coffee to keep herself awake.

Marjorie said she didn't know, but "she certainly was making something." After I returned home, I found that Mrs. Crenshaw had made herself some coffee during the evening (at about the time of Marjorie's purported visit) and as a sort of afterthought, quite contrary to her regular practice, had set out cups, saucers, plates and cereal dishes, so that they would be ready for our breakfast early the next morning.

In connection with this experiment, a question arose as to our "right of privacy" from inquisitive or even malicious spirit-entities who come close to the so-called physical plane. The answer was that neither our homes nor the psychic atmosphere (aura) of our individual person may be invaded by a spirit without invitation, either clearly expressed or implied by the quality of our thoughts.

Moreover, we were told that any person of good character is constantly protected by "guardian angels," who are either friends, relatives or "guides" attracted to us according to the state of our consciousness, and it is their duty not only to inspire us and help us by assisting in harmonizing our vibratory fields but also to guard us from unwarranted intrusions by undesirable entities.

In addition, it was explained that the observation of earth activities by persons in the next plane is not too easy. Always there is a "veil," a mist-like vibratory layer, which separates the spirit entity from the physical plane, and to "pierce the veil" can at times require real effort. On the other hand, persons having a low state of mind, such as those addicted to excesses of any kind, are liable to attract to themselves astral entities of a similarly low character, who feed their own starved appetites by attaching themselves to the vital or etheric body of the earth-person. There may, therefore, be unfortunate reactions as a result of the interaction of low mental forces.

The solution is to raise the state of the individual consciousness by cleansing one's thoughts of all tendency toward excesses, according to the teachers who have spoken through Richard Zenor. They have repeatedly emphasized the axiom that "like attracts like" and that the cleansing process of clear, harmonious thinking is a powerful agent for health, happiness and general well-being in both worlds.

THE COMMUNICATORS

II

WE HAVE BEEN SPEAKING mainly of those communicating spirits who are friends and relatives of the seeker after communication or other individuals using the instrument primarily for a social conversation and personal solace. If such were the only purpose of mediumship, our "telephone" would, of course, still be valuable. The propaganda value alone would be worth the effort—opposing such absurd notions as the immediate destruction of personality at death and the fear of eternal damnation, rather than rational retribution.

Yet the use of the instrument for these personal "contacts" is in reality a subordinate, if nevertheless important, part of its functions. More important is its use as a channel whereby we may learn more of the purposes of life, through a fuller understanding of the nature and relationship of the various phases of what we call the after-life. Obviously some are in a better position than others to introduce us to these mysteries, and it is fortunate that Richard Zenor is able to present himself as the kind of instrument which can be operated by many types of personalities.

In general, there are three classes of communicators through the mediumship of Mr. Zenor. First, there is the infinite variety of personalities which is similar to the classes and kinds of individuals we meet daily in this world. Second, there are the Master Teachers, who are individuals advanced so highly by reason of experience and unfoldment that they are able to instruct us properly and accurately concerning the nature of the after-life and our place in the plan of the universe. They are the initiates of the mysteries, the guardians of the ancient wisdom, who with simplicity and humility and with gentle tenderness attempt to light our way a little brighter along the road of life.

There is also a third, "in-between" group, composed of persons in the spirit world who do not differ essentially from those in the first class, except that their capacity to be messengers, helpers and inspirers in the spirit realms is greater than most, by virtue of their advancement to higher planes of consciousness. Some are "angels of light," to use an ancient term, who try to aid those in lower planes of the after-life and those still in the material world. They seek to alleviate suffering and disharmony by inspiring the individual to understand his problems in such a way that he will by his own efforts achieve peace and realization within himself. A vast array of specialist helpers likewise assists in the creative fields of art and industry by inspiring men to bring into material being works which will tend to advance their understanding, harmonize their experiences and expand their consciousness. Many organized orders of helpers and messengers exist in spirit, we are told, and any number of these bring forth messages of inspiration and information through appropriate channels.

It should not be assumed that there is little to learn from communicators who are not Master Teachers. Just as we can learn from those around us at any time, the average individual who speaks through mediumship usually has something to offer by way of information or inspiration that is valuable to us. But on basic philosophical questions his opinions are apt to be little better qualified than most persons living in the physical body. We will attempt to explain the reasons for this more fully later.

Meanwhile, we find that some of the not-so-advanced spirits can tell us a great deal concerning the mental and physical aspects—and, strangely enough, there are physical aspects—of the after-earth existence. They also can furnish us with convincing proof of the continuity of life. For instance, many years ago during my early acquaintance with Mr. Zenor, I witnessed this somewhat typical incident:

I had arranged for some friends to visit one of Mr. Zenor's meetings. They in turn brought another friend, a Mrs. H., to a subsequent meeting. None of these persons, therefore, knew the medium personally. Nevertheless, Mrs. H.'s father talked with her and identified himself by singing, in Dutch, a little song which she immediately recognized as one he had sung to her often when she was a child.

Another incident of the same general character is this one:

Mrs. R., a stranger to Mr. Zenor, was pleased when her mother spoke to her through the medium and addressed her as "Nell," the pet name which the mother had always used, though her real name was Eleanor. The mother further identified herself by exclaiming, "What

have you done with your beautiful hair?" Mrs. R. once
had very long hair, which she wound around her head
in a becoming style, but with the change in fashions had
long since cut it shorter. No one else present at the meeting could have known this, she said later.

Nor could anyone else have understood what happened
next. A man's voice greeted her, called her by her maiden
name and gave the name of the town in Scotland where
she had formerly lived. She knew it was her father, because all of the speech was in Gaelic, including the Gaelic
form of her name. She had been taught her name and
correct address as a child in case she ever were lost, and
her father was merely reminding her of the many times
he had impressed upon her the importance of learning
the Gaelic patter. The demonstration was doubly significant for Mrs. R., because her mother, who had just ceased
speaking through the instrument and was obviously witnessing this performance, had always ridiculed the idea of
learning the difficult Gaelic forms because she regarded
the old Scotch tongue as a dead language which few would
understand even if the little girl did become lost. (Details of this case are based upon my notes, recorded in
1937 when I investigated the matter.)

Following is a more recent case (1946):

During one of Mr. Zenor's mid-week meetings, a Mr.
M. talked with his mother in Spanish. She not only discussed personal matters which were not generally known,
but spoke with the kind of authentic Spanish accent characteristic of his mother and the district where she lived
in Mexico.

Here are the words which broke like an excited torrent
from the medium's lips:

"*¡Hijito!* (affectionate form of the word for son) *¡Cómo hacía que yo no hablaba contigo!* (How long it has been since I spoke with you!)

"*¡Ay, hijito! Estuviste muy malo, pero ya estas bien.* (Oh, son, you were very ill, but you are already well.)

"*Yo no te pude ayudar, pero la gente donde estas te ayudó mucho.* (I could not help you, but the people where you are helped you much.) *Estas muy bien donde estas ahora viviendo.* (You are very well where you are now living.)

"*Pero sigue con los tratamientos para la sangre.* (But continue the treatments for your blood.) *Ahora sí ya vas a estar bien.* (Now indeed you are going to be well.) *Ya no tienes que apurarte por nada porque estuviste muy malo.* (You no longer have to worry because you were so ill.)

"*Estan bien todos en casa.* (Everyone at home is well —referring to members of his family.)

"*Voy a la escuela.* (I am going to school.)

"*¡Vuelve!* (Come back!) *Adios.*"

Those who speak the language say that this is very typical Spanish as spoken by persons of Mexican origin, and the astonished Mr. M. insisted afterward that the accent and voice were typical of his mother during her lifetime. Moreover, the facts in her little speech were correct. He had been extremely ill but had practically recovered. He had recently changed his residence and was living with friends, who, indeed, were very helpful. Finally, it was true that he had been taking treatments which he himself called *tratamientos para la sangre.*

Mr. Zenor, so far as I have been able to determine, never has had an opportunity to learn any other language then English, and from my long observation of him,

I am convinced that he can speak no other language. But if he could, it would have been impossible for a native of this country to imitate so closely the distinctive accent of a woman from Mexico, say qualified observers who heard the demonstration. The fact that Mr. M., a stranger to the medium, had at a public meeting been called by his correct name when he was invited by the spirit "door-keeper" to speak with his mother is regarded as mere routine proof, although Mr. M. was further impressed by this detail.

But it was later when a brother also talked to him in Spanish through the medium that he was most impressed with the provable authenticity of the messages.

"¿Cómo estas, Huero?" said the voice through the instrument.

And by the one word "Huero" Mr. M. knew there could be no doubt that it was his brother speaking, for he had not been called "Huero" since his brother's death in Mexico ten years previously, and he had never been known by this nickname in the United States. The three Spanish words might be translated:

"How are you, Blondy"—except that huero used thus is a word peculiar to Mexico and refers not so much to the blonds of northern countries but to Latins who are lighter complexioned than their fellows. Since Mr. M. had the lightest hair and complexion of any member of his family in Mexico, this brother had always called him "Huero."

Many other examples of an evidential nature could be cited to illustrate the reliability of the instrument under favorable circumstances. In addition, the communicators include numerous speakers who are able to describe the conditions of the after-life existence. While these may not be so authoritative in their views and reports as the Master Teachers, nevertheless they bring through much that is of interest and value.

At one time during Mr. Zenor's career, a coterie of doctors communicated and lectured through him. In fact, the group was so predominant and the title "doctor" attached to so many speakers that the Navajo Indian "doorkeeper" for the medium decided he, too, should have a title. After all, was he not a medicine man for his tribe some 100 years back? Hence "Dr. Navajo," the medium's closest guardian, took his name and title.

It has been interesting to observe Dr. Navajo's development through the years. Originally, he spoke little English and the voice had a low gutteral quality. Neither could he control the medium's body, including the head, which lay on one side while he spoke. Gradually, however, as his control improved, so did his speech. Then slowly, almost imperceptibly, his voice came to sound much like Mr. Zenor's own voice—no doubt due to their close association for so long—and his English vocabulary and increasing breadth of expression began to show a deep understanding of the principles taught by the teachers. As he has said himself, he had been learning over there just as certainly, though with less distraction, as the students on this side.

Growth, both mentally and physically in the spirit world, has also been strikingly illustrated by another longtime collaborator with the medium. When I first heard her, Marjorie Keatland came through as a typical little girl of seven. Her voice, her vocabulary and her prankish whims and fancies were entirely in keeping with the outlook and character of a child of seven.

Significantly, her growth and her accumulation of a more sophisticated and expressive vocabulary were likewise almost imperceptible. Vocabulary growth was most noticeable when she would stumble over some new poly-syllabic word but would eventually master it and make it a permanent member of her language. After ten years, she exhibited the characteristics of a 'teen-ager almost grown. While such growth does not always proceed at the same rate as it does here, she was obviously no longer a child of seven (though her delightfully whimsical spirit still mani-fested itself and has been a constant attraction).

Others in the band of spirits who have worked regularly with Mr. Zenor at various times include individuals from many nations and many ages, singers as well as speakers, and it was not until the medium himself had gone through a long period of development and preparation that the Master Teachers began making use of his instrumentality.

Previously the student classes and lecture services had been in charge of preliminary teachers, who obtained their information in schools and institutions where the higher teachers were able to communicate directly with them. Most notable of the preliminary teachers was Dr. George Adams, who had been one of the early-day osteo-paths in Chicago.

Taking charge of a special class of students, he taught them much concerning the fundamental nature of the after-life and introduced them to the meaning and method of reincarnation, the cyclic unfoldment of the individual and spiritual development in general. Often his lectures would last for two and more hours, and question periods would produce lively discussions as he strove, with much success, to put into simple language the profound and, at times, seemingly inexpressible truths relating to the continuity and interrelatedness of all life.

❊❊❊❊❊❊❊❊❊❊❊❊❊❊❊❊❊❊❊❊❊❊❊

WHAT THE OTHER WORLD IS LIKE

❊❊❊❊❊❊❊❊❊❊❊❊❊❊❊❊❊❊❊❊❊❊❊

III

As with any instrument of communication, the use to which it is put may be either trivial or profoundly enlightening. Men of genius have exhausted their energies to create devices for the welfare of mankind, only to have their use abused in many instances by empty-heads who take for granted the convenience and good fortune bestowed on them by a beneficent society. Mediumship is no exception, although generally there is a systematic control exercised to prevent abuses which might otherwise discredit the instrument and bring hurt or harm to the user.

However, as in the case of any telephone, the kind of communications one receives depends in large measure upon the kind of person one is, which in turn governs the kind of persons one knows and would be apt to speak to over a telephone. Therefore, it is stupidly ignorant to blame the telephone for the kind of message that is transmitted. The message depends upon the person doing the communicating and is only modified to the extent that the instrument is not being operated efficiently.

Hence, if Grandpa tunes in from the astral world to

give an opinion exactly the opposite of that which Grandma expressed in a previous message, DON'T BLAME THE MEDIUM—any more than you would blame any telephone for the message it brings. The trouble is with Grandpa and Grandma, who very likely are just about the same kind of persons they were when they last departed from this mortal coil.

The frailties of humanity on whichever side of the veil they may be have been repeatedly demonstrated, and a good telephone can no more control the message or insure consistency with other transmitted messages than a postman can edit the mail. To illustrate:

At one of the Zenor meetings, a stranger was greeted by a feminine voice purporting to be that of the man's recently deceased wife. She immediately began to upbraid him for giving away some of her jewelry to another woman. The man walked out of the meeting, protesting that the accusation was a "damn lie." His opinion of the proceedings in general and the medium in particular was not any more tolerant.

Another husband, not a widower, visited the medium at a different time than his wife, with whom he was at odds over a domestic problem. Each received messages which were distinctly partisan and more or less conflicting, with the result that the husband promptly blamed the medium, rather than the communicators. I could as logically blame the telephone company for the conflicting stories I receive over my telephones practically every day (although the quality of the reception naturally depends upon the efficiency of the instrument used).

It is true that persons in the worlds of spirit grow, develop and advance, either as slowly or rapidly as their backgrounds and inclination will allow, but ordinarily and for quite a time after they cross over they are precisely the same individuals they were when they were on earth. They have the same likes and dislikes, the same prejudices and aversions, the same appetites and shortcomings, often the same occupations and more often the same religions.

The confusion on this point arises from a tendency—and escapist desire—to regard the immediate after-life state as being vastly different from the earthly state. It isn't. It is so exactly the same that it may literally be said to be painful—painful for those who have not cleansed themselves of complexes, phobias and fixations, hates, fears and frustrations, or even of petty worries and selfish preoccupations, BEFORE they leave the earthly "plane" of existence. Many observers and many communicators have written and spoken on this subject in many ages, and basically their concept of the after-life as being a continuation of the earthly life is the same. The principal difference, as we have said, is not of kind, but of degree: In the after-life world, the mental forces and their effects are paramount; that is, they are more immediate and more noticeable, as well as more acute, on the astral "plane" than they were on the earth plane. Only the dogma and doctrines of some theologians depart from this view, and even their interpretations are generally found to have their roots in reality. Many times the variances turn out to be mere variations, depending upon a specialized nomenclature (i.e., definitions of heaven, hell, purgatory, etc.) and a particular point of view, rather than a broad understanding of the whole picture.

Hence, we must avoid the common error of assuming that a person in spirit is all-knowing and all-wise, simply because the graduation exercise called death has promoted him to a new school of endeavor. That does not mean we should regard the communications from these recent "graduates" with either suspicion or distrust, but rather that they should be weighed and compared in the same way we would evaluate differing reports from visitors to a foreign land. Some are more authoritative than others. Some are more descriptive than others. Some are more general; some more specific and particularized. Some may be tainted with local superstitions and traditions. Some of the travelers may have journeyed far, and some may have been as isolated as a prisoner on an island. No two will tell exactly the same story, but from all will come a synthesis of information that by comparison and correlation can lead to greater understanding of the unseen land.

Fortunately, there is little disagreement among the communicators through Richard Zenor, due to the fact that his instrumentality seems to attract persons of understanding, both on this side and in the other world. Such disagreements as occur are more often concerned with mundane affairs than with spiritual explanations. The higher teachers have lead the way in the search for understanding, and they are generally restricted only by the limitations of language and not by a limited knowledge or wisdom. They do not pretend, of course, to be all-wise or all-knowing—for what soul can embrace all of the truth of which it is a part?—but their view of the laws and nature of the universe is bound to be clearer and more accurate than the reports of those who, with less assimilated experience, have not yet been graduated from the earth-projected spheres.

The God-consciousness, the Source of total wisdom, pervades all spheres, according to the teachings of the illumined ones. The light is filtered and diffused as it seems to leave a central source and is modified in the vibrations of materiality, but the heavenly messengers and their assisting entities work constantly to dispel the gloom —and this is a literal, as well as a figurative, concept—so that we all may grow toward the light according to our realization and understanding.

The mechanical and material aspects of the after-life, as we have stated, have caused considerable confusion among those who insist that spirit and spirituality must be totally divorced from form. In the planes immediately surrounding this earth, the two states are as interrelated, in a sense, as they are on the earth plane itself.

From the higher teachers, including not only those who are the source of so much inspiration through Mr. Zenor but others of many ages as well, we get this cosmological picture:

The earth is but one of countless inhabited planets, including some in our own solar system. Each planet is the central orb of a system of concentric spheres, the grossest and most crystallized of which is the material "plane" or surface of the planet. The spheres which enclose the planet vary in density according to the vibratory rate of each degree or plane and become less crystalline and more harmonious as to wave patterns as one proceeds outward from the planet's surface. The arrangement of the spheres or planes and their relation to each other is as precise and progessive as the electron fields of an atom or the periodic table of the elements.

Immediately surrounding the earth is a complex world called the "astral plane," and it is from dwellers in this world that we most often receive communications. Other planets have similar astral worlds, the nature of which depends upon the development of consciousness on the particular planet. Strictly speaking, the astral world is not a plane at all, but a series of planes or "degrees" of consciousness, beginning with a level some miles above the stratosphere. There the traveler in spirit will find the worlds of animals and plants, many now extinct on the earth plane. Even bacterial life has its astral habitat appropriate to its consciousness in the chain of evolution and its vibrational density.

Above the realms of the lower forms of life are the hell-like regions of abysmal darkness and the purgatorial regions of phobias, complexes and fixations inhabited by the "lost souls" from the earth plane—lost because they have not yet found themselves. It is understandable that these personalities are in darkness or in a dismal fog of suffering or despair when we realize that the environment of the astral world is one which readily reacts to mental impulses and is, in a sense, more of a mental world than the earth level.

Recognizing that we all are broadcasters of thought forces, having a vibratorial quality comparable to electromagnetic phenomena, one can easily imagine what the effect upon a susceptible environment would be if the impinging mental forces were disharmonious and confused. Light can only be produced by a complex of wave motions having a somewhat orderly pattern, and where the pattern is diffused and distorted by lack of order, relative darkness ensues. The individuals in these lower astral locations—which are also appropriately called "states of consciousness"—have actually created their hellish and purgatorial environments for themselves by the state of mind which they carried with them when they were released from their physical bodies.

In the after-life world, the discarnate personality gets

both what he expects and what he deserves. If he was of such a degraded intellect and criminal nature that his hatred of mankind fills his entire consciousness, undoubtedly he will gravitate to the regions of "outer darkness" appropriate to his thoughts. Especially will he find himself in darkness after he has throughly convinced himself by material living that there is no light or life in the afterworld. We are told that there are, quite literally, billions of these "lost souls," whose hates and lusts, supplementing each other, have created a veritable satanic hell—or series of inferno-like hells—from which they cannot escape, and even do not desire to escape, until they can somehow be awakened to the unnaturalness of their existence.

The purgatorial regions are thickly populated with individuals who are still so obsessed with their earthly concerns that they have re-created replicas of their own mental states and live, and suffer, in these states. The frustrated, the guilt-stricken, the phobia-ridden, the worriers, the haters, the revenge-seekers and the disillusioned all make their own little worlds, which overlap only insofar as the similarity of their mental depression-patterns or the history of their earthly experiences are closely interrelated.

For instance, the murderer overwhelmed with remorse will create his own ghostly punishment by imprisoning himself in his own thought-forms, which might be a constant re-enactment of his crime or a complete and vivid picturization of his own worst fears of adequate punishment. In another case, a woman long obsessed with the horror of growing old might find herself in an atmosphere of age and decay, with images of herself constantly mirrored before her, showing her beauty turning to ugliness.

The mean and petty gossip might create for herself a world in which she believes herself in a state of filth and degradation, brought on by her lust for mental dirt.

This is the law of attraction of the astral world, and of the earth and of the universe, too, say the teachers: No man is greater than himself, but always he must live with and within himself, and that which he thinks becomes his world, for he attracts to himself all that he is according to the degree of his consciousness.

These poor "sinners" of the lower astral are not being punished by God, but by themselves. And always the punishment perfectly fits the crime, for they have themselves judged themselves by the state of their consciousness, which suspends them in the infernal aura of their misdeeds or misapprehensions and frustrations until the weight of their experience has been absorbed and they can grow again toward the light. The principle does not change, either on earth or above earth, for we know that the composition of our thoughts is the composition of our private worlds, ranging accordingly from a state of happiness to one of despair, as we choose by our will, our learning and our understanding to make it so.

It is thus that we find in some of the higher degrees of the astral a fairly "normal" type of consciousness where comparatively well-adjusted people congregate in a social existence closely paralleling that of the earth plane. They have their cities, towns and villages, their homes, their buildings and their pursuits much like those in many sections of the earth world. They wear clothes, maintain their personality traits, have solid bodies and carry on their activities, to all intents and purposes much as they did before their passing from the earth sphere.

How is all this possible? To the student who can disabuse himself of the idea that a departed soul immediately upon leaving the earth enters a formless, completely spiritualized state, uncomplicated by material properties, the answer is no more obscure than the functioning of a radio set. Just as different broadcasting stations are tuned to various vibrational levels or "frequencies" of vibration, so the degrees and planes of the so-called immaterial worlds represent differing wave patterns and frequencies. However, they are immaterial only insofar as their crystalline properties are more directly affected by the mental and spiritual development of their inhabitants. That is why a location in the spirit world often is referred to as a "consciousness" by those on the other side. And, appropriately, they sometimes use the same term for locations on the earth.

All matter, in essence, is a complex of wave patterns, and the strata or layers of vibrational grouping surround the lowest level, the earth plane, in a rising order of increased frequency. For example, as a broad analogy, suppose our material world were entirely made up of wave lengths or vibrational frequencies of the order of X-rays— including bodies, trees, buildings, mountains and everything tangible to the five senses—, then we could assume that those in another world entirely made up of the slower, lower frequency vibrations of the order, say, of radio waves would be entirely unaware of their existence, unless the frequency gap were bridged by some device.

Consequently, the radio wave personality would be unable to gravitate to the X-ray world or see the forms made up of X-ray frequencies without a vital transformation, although the X-ray people could observe with some probable limitations the grosser forms of the slower radio wave world. The two worlds might even impinge and intermingle at times with only the X-ray people being aware of it. Those in the radio wave world would only be aware of such aberrations and departures from the normal as might cause minor disturbances in the vibrational sea of the radio wave lengths.

As a practical matter, each earth-form—in fact, each atom—is said to possess all of the various levels of vibration, and these are shed off, much like a snake sheds its skin, in the process of arising from the grosser planes to the higher. Hence, the physical body is only one of many bodies which an individual possesses; so upon leaving the physical shell, the individaul finds himself in an astral body that is a replica in all particulars of his physical self (often, however, minus illnesses and deformities, depending upon his state of consciousness) and which is completely substantial in the—to him—solid and substantial astral world. There are also spiritual bodies which vibrate according to the frequencies of still higher spheres, and it is the progressive refinement and manifestation of these higher bodies as the inherent wisdom of the soul is made objectively real through experience that we call "self-unfoldment." While unfoldment progresses, the density of the bodies automatically decreases, and the individual automatically "gravitates" to an environment that is congenial to his personal vibration pattern.

Astral communities closely correspond both in location and similarity to their counterparts on the earth plane. Unless they have attained unusual spiritual growth, a person from a particular city or country will gravitate to the counterpart of that city or country in the astral, and this location generally is directly over the original location on the earth. In the new environment, the graduated entity finds little changed, except that everything is greatly influenced by his thoughts. He can move by means of his thoughts and even construct quasi-material objects or structures—his home, for instance—with his thoughts, subject only to the restrictions of his natural skill to concentrate and visualize accurately.

By his mental force he can attract to himself from the lower degrees plants and animals which he wishes to have about him. The Indian literally has his Happy Hunting Ground and the religionist his particular brand of heaven. Others have their homes in communities which have developed by the gathering together of persons with resonant interests and thought-vibration patterns. Only the economic element is different. Since one may eat for pleasure but need not eat for survival, economic competition is eliminated, and such trade as there is in most states of astral consciousness reduces itself to a barter of skills. The skilled home-builder trades his services for a good suit of clothes, or maybe nothing but the fun of doing the job, for there is no lack of materials and supply in the mental worlds, where atomic force is everywhere available and can be molded by a thought.

Not only may the astral entity mold and attract to him that which his consciousness is able to conceive; he may also attract himself to different locations and degrees by re-tuning his basic frequency through the operation of the will. Thus, within limitations, he may rise to higher degrees temporarily by reducing his own density (but usually this is with the help of "messengers" and teachers from the upper planes) or he may descend to lower states of consciousness by reducing his basic frequency.

If he returns to the earth level, his active body, of course, will remain fundamentally composed of a wave pattern of a different order than that of his former earth-body.

Therefore, he will not be seen, felt or heard under ordinary circumstances by those whose consciousness is still limited by the highly crystallized material shell. He will be able to observe to a degree the places he visits on the earth plane, and like radio waves, his astral body, moved by his own will, can pass easily through the dense structures of the earth consciousness. His visitations then will be limited only by his will and the protective force thrown around the homes and persons of the "just" by the "guardian angels" of earth dwellers. The "just," it must be understood, however, include all persons, whether they are religious in the usual sense or not, whose mental makeup is such that they do not normally attract the "negative" forces of disharmony, hate, revenge, worry, fear, grief, venality, debauchery, plain selfishness, et cetera. (This, of course, is a vast subject, which can only be touched upon here.)

Given certain unusual conditions, astral entities may momentarily take on gross physical forms which make them temporarily solid to those of the earth consciousness. This may be due to the psychic history of a particular place, such as the scene of a crime which attracts the discarnate criminal and provides a vibrational field for the re-embodiment of himself and the forms associated with his guilt. Or, under certain circumstances, the density of the entity may be increased only sufficiently to affect material objects without his presence being seen. Poltergeist activity, the moving of objects by apparent immaterial means, is a form of this phenomena.

Certain types of mediums frequently provide ectoplasmic emanations and psychic force which can be used by astral entities to make themselves seen and heard when the conditions are favorable. Full-form materializations have often been seen in the presence of some mediums and have been photographed under the strictest test conditions, notably by the British scientist, Sir William Crookes, in the last century.

Is contact with persons from the astral world necessarily harmful or perilous? In general, it is not, any more so than contact with one's neighbors, friends and relatives—the plain, average people who make up the bulk of the population of both this world and the astral. There are, of course, mischievous and evil entities in the lower degrees of the astral, as well as earth-bound souls, who are capable of producing unfortunate reactions in the earth individual, but only if the psychic door is thrown open to them by the kind of negative thinking referred to above. The reasonably well-adjusted, good-humored, normal individual, who has "guardians" of like character, has nothing to fear so long as this balanced mental outlook is maintained.

One must remember, too, that there are higher degrees of spirituality in the astral world which partake of the fineness and beauty of the celestial sphere—the plane next above the astral. The middle astral degrees are the areas in which individuals and groups over many thousands of years have built up by their consciousness the replicas of their former earth homes. As one progresses toward the celestial, the material aspects of life tend to become more idealized, and activity is directed more toward the attainment of wisdom and realization concerning the meaning of existence.

The celestial plane is the abode of the heavenly messengers, "angels" of understanding and compassion, who work constantly to inspire those in lower levels to dispel the forces of disharmony around them and to arise higher and higher to a paradise of outward and inward beauty and understanding. These "angels" are not a special creation, but merely advanced souls who have acquired their compassion along the same road of experience and progression that all of us are traveling. They devote themselves largely to helping the ones who are behind them on the ladder of life. Through individuals on the earth plane with sufficient internal harmony to be impressed, they become sources of inspiration in the earth world.

The soul which arises above the paradise of the celestial plane finds himself in what is called the Cosmic Consciousness. As the name implies, this is the vibrational and spiritual level at which the individual becomes aware not only of the physical but the spiritual aspects of the cosmos. From there he may go to the myriad worlds of Immensity, the name given to the vast order of advanced states of consciousness completely beyond the influence of material planets. It is from certain degrees of consciousness on the "outer rim" of Immensity that the Agashan teachers and other Master Teachers dwell. There they are able to maintain themselves, because they have completely graduated from their long cycle of planetary lives and are in a position, by reason of their great learning and understanding, to assist others in reaching a similar consciousness.

In turn, they continue to advance toward what they term the "core" or "yolk" of life, the Absolute consciousness, a state which is, however, so ineffably and inexplicably beyond the comprehension of earthly mortals that attempts to describe it in the limited terms of an earth-limited language tend to be confusing rather than illuminating. Illumination is primarily a process of releasing the inward light of the soul into the objective consciousness, say the teachers, and this process of advancement, even in the infinite world of worlds that is Immensity, is measured according to our time, not in years, but in eons and ages, or a kind of timelessness broken by vast rhythmic growth and evolutionary change.

Needless to say, once the fetters of material limitations are broken so that the individual begins to understand the relationship of form to his existence and the significance of material experience, there is thereafter for him a measureless joy in living and a selflessness of expression that is truly heavenly. Rarely does the individual accomplish this emancipation while still living in the physical vehicle on earth; more often it occurs afterward and only following countless revolutions of the ego with as many different personality expressions as are necessary to stimulate unfoldment.

All things, from the tiniest to the greatest, have their extensions into the infinite source, the all-pervading Oneness, the Universal Consciousness, say the teachers, so that all things and all beings are in reality a part of one another, affected by one another, dependent upon one another and are equally important to one another and to the consciousness we call God.

SOME COMMUNICATIONS

IV

IN WEIGHING the authenticity of "telephone" messages purporting to be from another world, the laboratory investigator seldom chooses or is able to evaluate certain subtle aspects which an unbiased jury might properly consider under the rules of evidence. The technician just as properly rejects them in the pursuit of his research, unless he is prepared to expand the rules of his field.

At a trial, the judge or jury is entitled to consider not only the objectively observed facts as reported by the witnesses and submitted in the form of documents and stipulations but is also empowered to consider a number of more subjective factors in determining whether the witnesses or documents have correctly pictured the facts. For instance, a witness's facial expressions, his manner of speaking, the readiness or slowness of his replies and his entire demeanor may be weighed in deciding whether or not he is telling the truth or whether—assuming his honesty—the circumstances of his observations have influenced him to color the facts.

Likewise, the circumstances surrounding the writing or production of documentary evidence often are considered in order to reach a conclusion, either as to the authenticity or accuracy of what they pretend to represent. A photograph may be offered into evidence without sufficient showing that it correctly represented a scene at the time in question, but the judge may deduce from the nature of the photograph or other available data that the representation is correct.

Late in 1947 I supervised the wire-recording of an entire message meeting, a regular mid-week public service, at which Richard Zenor, according to his custom, offered himself primarily as a "telephone" for personal communications by any and all who might be present. Since a large part of his other work consisted of lectures from the higher teachers, who used him more as a broadcasting instrument than a telephone, a regular weekly meeting had been set aside to permit those who desired to do so to make individual "contacts" with friends and relatives.

The recording was designed to preserve a truly typical and usual series of messages of the same general pattern I had heard for years through the instrument. No search was being made for outstanding bits of evidence or for unusual communications. In this case, I was seeking a record of what was average and ordinary. Yet typical as was the meeting on this particular occasion, there were two conversations in which foreign languages were spoken (Spanish and Italian). At the same time, the very artlessness and distinctively personalized quality of many of the messages could not fail to impress an unprejudiced judge. By all the standards of law, he could assume from the context of the conversations themselves that they were unacted, spontaneous and, therefore, sincerely evidential.

Consider this excerpt from a typewritten transcript of the recording—the first of the evening's messages:

MALE VOICE (through medium): The first vibration comes here—Louise wants to speak to Amelia.

WOMAN FROM AUDIENCE: Hello, darling.

FEMALE VOICE (through medium): I was over there today. I went over to the house, and I see you are preparing for Christmas and having a lot of fun, too. I think it is wonderful, don't you? You know that we can all be inspired around this time of year, and we are going to enjoy ourselves over here also. You know, we celebrate, too. We have a good time over here and try to come as close to the earth plane as we can to help those who are seeking, you know.

WOMAN: I am celebrating, too.

FEMALE VOICE: I think it is quite remarkable. You enjoy yourself and know that I am working with you and helping in every way I possibly can, because it is going to be a wonderful thing for you, and you must know that. I am going to work and bring forth all that is good, and I know I am just helping you—that is the main thing. God love you, darling.

Contrast this with the following colloquy, recorded a few minutes later:

MALE VOICE: The next vibration is Aunt Tillie who wants to speak to Ben. She calls you "Benjamin." Is that right?

YOUNG MAN FROM AUDIENCE: Yes, that is right.

MALE VOICE: Does she always call you Benjamin?

YOUNG MAN: Yes.

FEMALE VOICE: Hello, darling. Don't you wish I could make you some beautiful hot biscuits tonight? Remember my biscuits?

YOUNG MAN: Do I!

FEMALE VOICE: I made some wonderful biscuits for you, and you told me how you enjoyed them.

After some further conversation between these two about a person they called "Glen," the young man designated as Benjamin asked—

YOUNG MAN: Is Glen here?

MALE VOICE: Hi, pal.

YOUNG MAN: Hello, there. How are you?

MALE VOICE: I am sure tickled pink to come in and talk to you. By golly, we ought to do like you and I used to do—hike up in the Hollywood Hills. It would be a pretty good thing, don't you think? You know what? I am interested in aviation over here. I am sure doing fine. I have a lot of ideas I have been trying to cook up over here. They are my own ideas, and I don't know yet whether they are going to be of any value. I feel there is a lot of good ideas coming out in the next [several words indistinguishable]. It sure is nice as far as I am concerned, that so many nice things are being created on earth. I bet anything in a couple of years there will be more things on the earth than you could shake a stick at.

YOUNG MAN: They are working on a thing now to overcome gravity so the ships won't fall to earth. They are working on it now.

MALE VOICE: Gee, that is swell. How is television getting along?

YOUNG MAN: Pretty clear now.

MALE VOICE: I can remember when I heard a squeak on a radio, I thought I had something.

YOUNG MAN: I remember when I stood on the corner

and listened to the Jack Dempsey and Gene Tunney fight.

MALE VOICE: I used to do the same thing. I guess cars are some humdingers now, aren't they?

YOUNG MAN: Yeah. They are going to bring out a new one without any clutch, no transmission, no differential, and the motor in the rear. Boy, it's really going to be something. . . .

In all of these conversations, except as noted below, I did not know any of the persons speaking. Whether the medium was acquainted with them, I cannot say, but from the standpoint of credibility, I doubt that it is important. The record speaks for itself.

The study of literary styles is so formalized that college students often are asked to identify the author of a particular quotation merely from the style of writing, rather than from the subject matter quoted. Here are some further excerpts—all taken from the transcript of the one message meeting—which are interesting from the standpoint of differences in speaking style:

MALE VOICE (through medium): Good evening, my blessed child.

WOMAN FROM AUDIENCE: Good evening.

MALE VOICE: I am grateful to have this opportunity to manifest to you tonight.

WOMAN: I am so glad to have you come.

MALE VOICE: I know what you are doing in your unfoldment. There is one thing I would suggest to you, my child. Do not let conditions there in your work disturb you as they have. It has been very disturbing to you.

WOMAN: Yes, I know.

MALE VOICE: I don't want you to feel that way.

—51—

WOMAN: I think things are going to be worked out.

MALE VOICE: You must try to learn, my child, that you are on the earth plane, and people are the same the world over. They are disturbed, and if you let them bother you, you will be disturbed too. You must rise above that. You must rise above all talk that is negative and become attuned to the consciousness that dwells within. Then you will be able to understand that God is with you at all times and assisting you on the path. I am proud of you, however. Know that I come to you to show you the way and to help you to live the life I want you to live.

WOMAN: Bless you.

MALE VOICE: I give you my blessings. I will be with you tonight and every night when you call upon me and show you the way.

WOMAN: Thank you very much for all of your help.

MALE VOICE: I am sending you all the light I can. God bless you, my child.

* * *

MALE VOICE: Hello, this is Cappy. . . .

WOMAN FROM AUDIENCE: How have you been?

MALE VOICE: I have been fine. I didn't know whether I was supposed to come back here or not, or go on to another consciousness, but I like coming back, and I suppose that is why I hang around.

WOMAN: You do whichever is best for you.

MALE VOICE: I suppose I will have to go on. Some of the teachers over here think I should go on. I suppose I will have to go through a period of wanting to know what everything is about on the earth plane. . . . They tell me I have a lot to learn. Well, I imagine that is right. I used to think I knew it all when I was on earth, but I changed my mind since I came over here. Well, I am glad to be here and talk to you. I won't take any more of your time. I enjoyed talking to you.

* * *

MALE VOICE (to man and woman from audience): Gladys has been worrying about her daughter, I notice, and every time I contact her, it seems to me she is perturbed over some of the actions of the daughter. I suppose she will have to overcome that, or she will be helped if she has a willingness to be helped. . . .

* * *

MALE VOICE: There is a spirit here by the name of Elva asking for Ida.

WOMAN FROM AUDIENCE: Hello, Elva.

FEMALE VOICE: Hello, hello. How is our boy tonight?

WOMAN: He is fine.

FEMALE VOICE: I think he is beginning to realize things, and I think he knows I am beginning to work with him. I am not around him all the time, you know, because I am going to school, and I don't get an opportunity to stay so close to the earth all the time, but I am happy to know that we can at least have an occasional visit.

WOMAN: He always asks about you.

FEMALE VOICE: I know he does. I think he will be all right, because he is learning. Sometimes he has to learn the hard way, but he will get there.

WOMAN: He will, I know.

FEMALE VOICE: He loves you so dearly, and I do appreciate and thank you for all the good you are doing him.

WOMAN: I appreciate your coming.

FEMALE VOICE: It is truly wonderful. I believe as we go on that we will all be able to help one another.

WOMAN: I think so too.

FEMALE VOICE: Don't be too concerned about the children, because I think they will see things different as time goes on.

WOMAN: I don't bother about that. I am trying to forget it.

FEMALE VOICE: I realize that, and I think that is the way it is going to be for us.

*   *   *

MALE VOICE: How is Fritz feeling?

WOMAN FROM AUDIENCE: He is better, but, my, he looks awful bad.

MALE VOICE: He is looking bad and getting weaker because he has violated the law.

WOMAN: Yes, he is awfully weak.

MALE VOICE: I think he is beginning to realize this cannot go on. I think just as soon as he comes to a realization that the more you punish your body, the more suffering he is going to have to endure.

WOMAN: Do you think I should stay or go with him.

MALE VOICE: I am going to be perfectly frank with you. It doesn't make any difference whether you go or not, because you are perfectly safe—because we don't have any fear in our hearts. Personally I don't think if he keeps on that way he will be able to go, because the way he is carrying on he won't be strong enough. You can't dissipate like that. But, anyhow, you are feeling better, and that is more important to you. You know that yourself. A better thought about it, anyhow. Well, I am going to be frank with you. I suggest that you don't go. There is nothing wrong, but you know from your past experiences that they always have been the same, and I wouldn't get mixed up in that if I were you. That is my true thought from this side.

WOMAN: I don't know whether it would make me feel better to go away and get away from everything.

MALE VOICE: Well, it would be nice for you to go away and enjoy yourself under other arrangements.

WOMAN: I just don't know what to do, but I will do what I think is best.

MALE VOICE: I certainly will help you—you know that.

WOMAN: I want to thank you for all you have done.

MALE VOICE: Don't worry, because there is no percentage in that.

*　　*　　*

MALE VOICE: Hello. (Some words in foreign language) I no dead! I no dead!

WOMAN FROM AUDIENCE: You no dead.

MALE VOICE: I am alive!

WOMAN: I never expected you. I thought you were still alive.

MALE VOICE: I alive now, *si!* I am not sick any more. I am not lonesome any more.

(Additional conversation in foreign language)

MALE VOICE: I come to your *casa.*

WOMAN: You come back, *si?*

MALE VOICE: Not much trouble like before. All gone now. All trouble gone. Goodnight.

Such conversations, redolent with sincerity and patently ingenuous, are typical of thousands which have come through the same lips and the same vocal cords over a long period. They have the same flavor as ordinary telephone conversations—at least, long distance 'phone calls. Yet in them one will often find the kind of evidential material, spontaneously evoked without coaching or prompting, that a judge or jury might well consider relevent to the case for inter-world communication. Following are some further examples from the same evening's transcript—excerpts which contain references to private matters that obviously concern only the persons speaking and sound as though we had tuned in on a series of private telephone conversations:

MALE VOICE: You are doing what you are supposed to do at this time. I think you will sleep much better tonight. I know you appreciate that statement because sometimes you do get distressed at night, I notice. But don't be disturbed. You will sleep better tonight.
WOMAN FROM AUDIENCE: That is good.

*   *   *

MALE VOICE: It is Dad. Can you hear me?
MAN FROM AUDIENCE: Oh, yes, Dad.
MALE VOICE (jokingly): You wanted to keep me out of here tonight?
MAN: No, I should say not.
MALE VOICE: You don't think Francis is any more important than me, do you?
MAN: Oh, no!
MALE VOICE: I am glad to be here anyhow.
MAN: I want you to come any time you can.
MALE VOICE: Sadie is here. Sally is here. Elizabeth is

here. In fact, they are all here, but they can't all talk to you. They don't have time. We are all here anyhow.

*   *   *

MALE VOICE: The next vibration here is Mother asking for Mabel.

WOMAN FROM AUDIENCE: Hello, Mother dear.

FEMALE VOICE: Hello, my girl. Sometimes it is a little difficult to control, but I am grateful to be here tonight.

WOMAN: I am so happy you are here.

FEMALE VOICE: Have you heard from Mary?

WOMAN: Yes, I heard from her. I thought maybe she was fooling about coming.

FEMALE VOICE: No, she is not trying to fool you, darling. I know she isn't. She may come any time, you know. She has been thinking about it, but I guess that man is pretty sick. You have a happy Christmas.

WOMAN: I am very popular.

FEMALE VOICE: How do you like your new little home?

WOMAN: I just love it.

FEMALE VOICE: You have everything fixed up very nice.

WOMAN: There isn't much more I can do to it.

FEMALE VOICE: No, I don't think there is.

WOMAN: I am so grateful to talk to you.

FEMALE VOICE: Yes, I know. Maybe Marian will come and talk to me sometime. Wouldn't that be nice? (Some indistinguishable whispering) That would be wonderful. I am very happy, and I will come again. Good night, dear.

—57—

*   *   *

MALE VOICE: Hello, this is Con.

WOMAN: Hello, Con.

MALE VOICE: You are not surprised to hear from me, are you?

WOMAN: No, I am not.

MALE VOICE: John is with me tonight. He is laughing at me, and he said to ask you if you want to buy any groceries.

WOMAN: No, tell him I am going out.

MALE VOICE: He says he is not in the grocery business any more.

WOMAN: No, I am not either.

MALE VOICE: He says you and he had a lot of fun when you were in the grocery business.

WOMAN: Yes, we did.

MALE VOICE: Well, those days are over for you anyhow.

WOMAN: That is right. We will see better days.

MALE VOICE: Well, I think so. I just wanted to come in and say hello to you.

WOMAN: That's fine.

*   *   *

MALE VOICE: The next vibration is the spirit of Bob, who wants to speak to Agatha.

WOMAN FROM AUDIENCE: Hello, Bob.

NEW MALE VOICE: Hello, how are you? I wish you would tell Alice I come around a lot.

WOMAN: I think she knows it.

MALE VOICE: Sometimes she gets so disturbed I can't reach her.

WOMAN: I know that is right. She is awfully nervous. I told her you had been asking about her, and she said she would be out and try to contact you. She had been feeling you around at night a lot. She said she could feel you around.

MALE VOICE: Well, anyhow, give her my love, won't you?

WOMAN: She will contact you after the first.

MALE VOICE: I will tell you one thing though. I think it was awfully silly for them to bring my body across from over there. Of course, we have different ideas when we get over on this side. All that trouble of bringing the body back here! What good is it anyhow? I am not conscious of it any more. It is just like a dirty old shirt as far as I am concerned.

WOMAN: But you know how your mother feels.

MALE VOICE: Mother feels that way, and I guess everybody else does, but I sure don't any more.

WOMAN: I know. It isn't hard for me to understand, but she couldn't.

MALE VOICE: Well, it's all right.

WOMAN: She wants her to come down when your body comes back.

MALE VOICE: Uh-huh. I don't know whether Alice will be well enough for that. I don't know. She isn't very well. From the looks of things she isn't thinking quite right either.

WOMAN: No, I know she isn't.

MALE VOICE: Well, I hope she can change her thoughts. I sure appreciate coming in and talking to you.

WOMAN: I sure appreciate it, too.

MALE VOICE: Give her my love, won't you?

WOMAN: Yes, sure I will.

*　　*　　*

FEMALE VOICE: How are you, pappy?

MAN FROM AUDIENCE: Okay, darling.

FEMALE VOICE: If I couldn't come and talk to you, I would be disappointed. . . . When I am talking to you, I am happy about it. I think I will have to go with you on the airplane trip. [Note: No previous mention of any kind of trip.]

MAN: Yeah, you do that. The big chief said he would go along, too. . . .

FEMALE VOICE: Don't forget the password.

MAN: Manzahalla.

FEMALE VOICE: No. What we said on the earth plane —"Give me a smootch."

MAN: Oh, that is right. Good night, darling.

*　　*　　*

MALE VOICE: Here is Aunt Goldie, who wants to speak to Hazel.

FEMALE VOICE: Hello there!

WOMAN FROM AUDIENCE: Hello, Aunt Goldie.

FEMALE VOICE: Can you hear me, dear?

WOMAN: Oh, yes; wonderfully well.

FEMALE VOICE: Vern is here, too.

WOMAN: Bless his heart.

FEMALE VOICE: He seems to be enjoying his music so much. He is going on with it the way he used to. He is trying to help others to progress in that field too, and I think that is wonderful, don't you?

WOMAN: Yes, indeed.

FEMALE VOICE: I told him he would be a director of music some day. He said he thought maybe he would. You know, he can go on with his music over here, just like he did on earth.

WOMAN: Yes, I know. That is just fine.

FEMALE VOICE: It is wonderful to know that it can come along that way. Mother is doing fine also. She seems to be accepting some of the things that are taught, oh, yes, but over here it is just like on the earth plane— we get somewhat disturbed about things that are brought to our attention, because we don't change much when we come out of the body, but I am very happy to be here and talk to you.

WOMAN: I am so glad to talk to you.

* * *

MALE VOICE: The next vibration is a spirit by the name of Kelly who wants to speak to Mary.

NEW MALE VOICE: Hello there! I am able to manifest tonight, too. You know, it seems a little strange at first to be able to control the instrument, but I am here just the same.

WOMAN FROM AUDIENCE: That's good.

MALE VOICE: Know that I am coming along like you want me to over here.

WOMAN: Wonderful!

MALE VOICE: I was wondering if you want to leave the place where you are, because I kept picking up your thought that you would like to go away. The thing to do right now is to carry on your spiritual work and that will bring about the conditions that you want on the earth plane.

WOMAN: I think so too, darling.

MALE VOICE: I wouldn't worry about it. I know there will be a way for you.

WOMAN: Yes, I am sure of that.

MALE VOICE: Well, you know how I have been. I was over in the office with you, too. I know you haven't been very well satisfied over there. You get yourself straightened around, and I am working with you the way you want me to or the way you want, too, rather.

WOMAN: Yes, it is wonderful.

MALE VOICE: I am not suffering now. You know that. I am freed from all that worry, and I know what you were going through with the trouble with your teeth.

(Some indistinguishable whispering.)

MALE VOICE: Know that I am guiding you and helping you from this side. I wish you could see some of the beautiful things over on this side. It makes us happy to know that God is with us all the time and all we have to do is to recognize Him. It means a lot to us.

WOMAN: It certainly does. How is Dad getting along?

MALE VOICE: Oh, just wonderful. It does me so much good to talk to him. He is beginning to realize a lot of things that he didn't understand on the earth plane.

WOMAN: You tell him I love him a lot.

MALE VOICE: We all send you our love from this side. . . .

*   *   *

MALE VOICE: The next vibration here is a spirit by the name of Gene, who wants to speak to Betty.

NEW MALE VOICE: Hello, there!

WOMAN FROM AUDIENCE: Hello, darling.

MALE VOICE: We are all very happy to be here tonight to contact you. Isn't that wonderful. It seems wonderful to manifest through the instrument and talk to you.

WOMAN: Yes, isn't it!

MALE VOICE: I wish you knew how happy I am and how well I am doing over on this side.

WOMAN: I know you are.

MALE VOICE: Harold is doing nicely. He is supposed to be coming along nicely. Well, I want to see him get himself straightened out, and I know that he is going to be absolutely all right.

WOMAN: Well, you are helping him. Your spirit is helping him wonderfully. I can tell it, too. I feel you around the room all the time.

MALE VOICE: Well, I presume so. I have a reason to be there. I came over today, and I saw you reading. You have just about finished that book. You liked it very much. I have been looking over your shoulder to see what it is all about.

WOMAN: I want you to read that book, because it is very good.

MALE VOICE: It helps you to understand things you are doing and what we have over here on this side. Of course, there are so many ways of expressing that, you know.

WOMAN: I know.

MALE VOICE: It seems to me that you are managing to come along good in your unfoldment, as long as we stay on the path, and that includes me on this side, too.

WOMAN: Agasha is giving us a wonderful study here.

MALE VOICE: Yes, it is a wonderful study. . . . You know how we used to do when I was on the earth plane. Things we had to go through and all the sorrow and all the things the folks used to say about us, and we went on just the same, didn't we?

WOMAN: You bet we did, and we still go on. The only thing that separates us now— It won't be long now.

MALE VOICE: I would like to see Harold get himself straightened around. I believe everything will be all right.

WOMAN: You know that old saying, "It won't be long now"—you used to say that.

BOTH: (Laughter)

*   *   *

MALE VOICE: The next vibration is Mother asking for Ruth. Also there is a sister here by the name of Jenny.

FEMALE VOICE: Hello, this is Jenny.

WOMAN FROM AUDIENCE: Hello, Jenny; how are you?

FEMALE VOICE: Mother is here, too, but I thought I would come in first. You know, sometimes when I control the instrument, it seems like I am right back on earth, and I see you so gorgeous. I see you so clearly tonight. It is just wonderful. I think Henry is coming along fine, too. He is beginning to realize a lot of things he didn't understand before.

WOMAN: Is he going to accept this religion like I have?

FEMALE VOICE: I am sure he will come to it. He may find it difficult to understand—that is why they don't accept it. They don't realize many truths can come. All the truths can come from the higher planes over here, because the teachers are wonderful, and they are doing everything they can to make it possible to help people in the earth plane. You understand, but there are a lot of people who won't understand at all.

WOMAN: I understand. It's my religion, darling.

NEW FEMALE VOICE: Hello, darling.

WOMAN: Hello, Mother.

FEMALE VOICE: I am very grateful to be here to talk to you tonight, too.

WOMAN: How are you tonight? I am happy to have an opportunity to talk to you.

FEMALE VOICE: I am just fine, and it certainly is wonderful to come back to talk to you. Did you know I saw you this morning when you were drinking coffee?

WOMAN: Yes, I saw your light.

FEMALE VOICE: Do you know what you said?

WOMAN: I said, "Mother, are you here?"

FEMALE VOICE: Yes; then you walked over to the stove and came back and sat down. You could just almost see me sitting at the opposite side of you.

WOMAN: Mother, I was so grateful to get your vibration.

FEMALE VOICE: Tell Henry I said hello.

WOMAN: Thank you, darling.

FEMALE VOICE: Know that I am not suffering at all. We like to come back to tell you we haven't any aches or pains over here.

WOMAN: It is wonderful.

FEMALE VOICE: Good night, and bless you.

It is notable that throughout the transcript of this one evening's messages there was no prying or coaching on the part of the communicators at any time—no attempting to obtain information by adroit questions or searching hints. Rather, the inclination was exactly opposite: to give evidential information and clues in a most natural fashion; that is, without any thought of evidence.

And I can testify that the conversations recorded on this single night were entirely typical of the style and content of thousands of messages transmitted through this "telephone" down through the years. Where satisfactory contact is made—and this is not to say that all "contacts" are satisfactory, for there are rules and conditions which must be satisfied, just as in the case of any other mechanism of communication—the conversation almost inevitably falls into a pattern not unlike the average long distance telephone call between friends and relatives still in the body.

How very naturally those who have used the instrument regard its use, no matter how well they may know the personality of Richard Zenor, is illustrated by the following conversation between his wife, Mrs. Thelma Zenor, and an entity speaking through her husband's lips and recorded for the same transcript:

MALE VOICE: Hello—[this is] Pop!

MRS. ZENOR: How are you, Pop?

MALE VOICE: You went down to Mom's today, didn't you?

MRS. ZENOR: Yes, I went down there.

MALE VOICE: I was down there, too, and I saw you.

MRS. ZENOR: Did you hear us talking?

MALE VOICE: Yes—quite a conversation.

MRS. ZENOR: Wasn't it though!

BOTH: (Laughter)

MALE VOICE: There was a lot of truth in what you said.

MRS. ZENOR: What do you think about that lady?

MALE VOICE: I was quite surprised when I heard you say she is interested in spiritualism.

MRS. ZENOR: Yes, after all these years, it comes out!

MALE VOICE: It is something to think about. It shows how many people are interested in it and won't say anything about it. Well, after all, I didn't know anything about it. I didn't pay any attention. I thought it was all a lot of bunk.

MRS. ZENOR: I know; that is what the majority of people think.

MALE VOICE: But you have to die first to find out the truth of things.

MRS. ZENOR: A lot of people don't—

MALE VOICE: Well, I did.

MRS. ZENOR: I know you did. Are you glad now?

MALE VOICE: Yes, I am glad now. But it takes time, I guess, for us to realize what it is all about. Well, I am glad you went to see Mom. Everything is all right, and I will be with you again, and good night, dear.

MRS. ZENOR: Good night, Pop.

An attorney read the record of this one night's messages and then mentally added to it the thousands of other messages, lectures and demonstrations which had flowed through Richard Zenor in an uninterrupted stream for so long. Then he commented:

"To assume that one mind could produce such an incredible variety of information and wide range of personality transformations is to sanction a miracle far less reasonable and more unnatural than if we accept them at their face value as communications from another world. Even if we make the impossible assumption that Richard Zenor had some secret access to the information relating to those for whom he is an instrument, the constant use of proper names correctly and in proper relation to the facts would imply that he possessed a miraculously phenomenal and agile memory, entirely beyond the capacity of ordinary men."

My own observation of Richard Zenor is that he is an ordinary man in the sense that he has his own likeable, distinctively human personality, not very different from the "average" American, but that he is extraordinary in his capacity to make himself a reliable "telephone between worlds."

TESTING THE SPIRITS

V

> Beloved, believe not every spirit, but try the spirits whether they are of God; because many false prophets are gone out into the world.
> —I John IV: 1

ONE OF THE MOST venerated tenets of the orthodox doctrine of science is that one laboratory experimenter upon duplicating the work of another should achieve the same or similar results to prove a generalized conclusion. In other words, if white mice are inoculated with a certain identifiable virus in one laboratory and come down with a palsy, white mice similarly inoculated in another laboratory should do the same. This, after repeated trials, would justify the conclusion that the virus was the cause of the symptoms.

Obviously it is impractical and ordinarily impossible to subject the phenomena of communication to that kind of testing, but in 1947 something of a three-way interlocking experiment—an unplanned, spontaneous experiment —occurred which approached the requirements of an unreconstructed scientist.

First, Juliette Ewing Pressing and her husband, Ralph G. Pressing, editors of the Psychic Observer, received at their office in Lily Dale, N.Y., a series of pastel drawings sent to them by S. A. Macdonald, psychic artist of 27a Addison Gardens, London W. 14, England. He said they had been sketched and colored from clairvoyant visions of the spirit personalities represented. The series included an American Indian called "White Feather" and a Chinese whose name was given as "Chang Foo Li."

Shortly after receiving the pictures, Mr. and Mrs. Pressing flew to California, but had mentioned nothing of the drawings to anyone other than their office staff; nor did they mention them further or publish any matter relating to them until after the "laboratory demonstrations" which they encountered in California.

The first demonstration occurred in San Francisco while the two noted editors were "telephoning" the other world through the mediumship of Florence Smith Becker, 194 Brentwood Avenue, San Francisco. Wrote Mrs. Pressing later:

"After others had expressed their greetings, a most dramatic entree was made which proved to be a most powerful spirit. The room—walls, chairs, floor—vibrated as though a slight earthquake might be taking place. Then a strong resonant Indian voice spoke, saying:

" 'I am White Feather. I posed for my portrait with an artist in England. I am well satisfied with the results. I have come to bring power and peace. There is great work to be done.' "

A few days later, Mr. and Mrs. Pressing witnessed the second private demonstration, this time in the little church known as the Agasha Temple of Wisdom in Los Angeles, with Richard Zenor acting as the "telephone." In the May 25, 1947, issue of the Psychic Observer, they reported:

"For almost three hours, no less than two dozen spirits

manifested through the trance mediumship of Rev. Zenor. Many of the controlling entities were the medium's own spirit teachers and collaborators; others were spirit people directly associated with the sitters, but the most conclusive evidence received was when the editors heard a certain Chinaman speak, first in Chinese, then in broken English.

"He proved his identity by linking up his message with a certain pastel drawing. This pastel, a likeness of the Chinese who spoke, was made in England by the London psychic artist, S. A. Macdonald, and was received by the editors a few days before they left Lily Dale on their California trip.

"Through Rev. Zenor, this Chinaman spoke of 'his picture, described the coloring and explained how he was able to impress the artist and how pleased he was with the result. No part of this message could possibly have been known by the medium; no one had seen the picture of the Chinaman except the editors, who at the time had never heard of him . . . and then to have the picture and the Chinaman's name corroborated was, in itself, a most conclusive bit of evidence."

In the June 25, 1947, issue of the Observer, Mr. and Mrs. Pressing reproduced the series of drawings, including the likenesses of White Feather and Chang Foo Li. Concerning the latter, the Observer reiterated:

"Rev. Zenor could not possibly have known about the picture. The Chinaman gave his name and described his own picture in detail—one of the most evidential messages ever received by the editors."

One of the most curious of the ancillary types of phenomena which often accompany inter-world communication is the stubborn refusal of some otherwise sincere investigators to accept any part of the theory of spiritism, even in the face of overwhelming evidence. Not only do they frequently invent the most outlandish and illogical conjectures to discredit the observed facts, but there have been instances in which the supposedly scientific investigator has resorted to fraud in an attempt to prove his contention of fraud in the production of the phenomena.

I know of no such extreme case relating to the work of Richard Zenor, but the obstinate tendency toward nonacceptance of even the hypothetical possibility of communication is very often noticeable among persons who are impatient of the unspectacular or who are hopelessly convinced of the inviolability of matter. They feel perfectly justified in looking the psychic creature straight in the face and pronouncing finally and irrevocably, "There's no such animal!" Fortunately, leading thinkers are gradually making this point of view socially, as well as scientifically, unpopular, and many who boast of being "liberals" in their thinking are discovering that they are on the unliberal, conservative, "reactionary" side when they categorically reject the voluminous proofs of spiritism.

Apparent flaws in the theory and seeming inconsistencies in the proofs likewise impress such closed minds as constituting an incontrovertible argument against the validity of the phenomena, while more patient researchers and observers attempt to probe further into the mystery in search of more complete answers to the paradoxes. They know that it is quite usual for inconsistencies to show up in any investigation, scientific or otherwise, and in fact would regard it unnatural were it otherwise. The gaps can never be filled in all at once, and the unnaturalness of a too-perfect case should be cause for suspicion, rather than conflict in the preliminary findings.

I am sure a good friend will forgive me if I cite her experience as an example of the tendency by some to reject evidence on purely arbitrary grounds. It was in 1938 that Miss Mercer, as I will now call her, and I attended a Zenor class in which a speaker discussed the problem of symbols and the significance of their use in communication. Finally, he spoke to each of the group present in turn, describing, as he said, one or more symbols that had formed etherically in the room—and seemed to be associated with whichever person was being addressed.

Coming to Miss Mercer, he described several images which, he stated, appeared to be associated with her in some way. First, there was a "black cow," the significance of which he said he could not understand. Next, there was a "gold comb," and he told her:

"It seems like someone has some jewelry that belongs to your mother—that your mother never received."

Finally, there was a casket, which he stated indicated that some relative would die soon—a distant relative, whose death would not greatly affect her.

Meanwhile, at the beginning of the discussion the speaker had remarked:

"There is [the etheric image of] a big red apple in the middle of the floor. I don't know who it belongs to."

As the meeting was about to close, Miss Mercer suddenly remembered a long-forgotten incident and interrupted.

"Wait! Wait!" she cried. "How about the big apple in the middle of the floor?"

It was still there, the communicator replied, adding:

"And I think it is for you."

Miss Mercer then wanted to know, "Who is giving it to me?"

"Wait a minute," said the voice through the medium. And after a pause: "There is somebody with a long black robe like a priest." Excitedly, the young woman asked for the name of the priest, and the communicator said he would try to get it for her—at least, the initials. Miss Mercer said later she realized that initials would mean nothing to her, because she could not remember the name herself—except that the proper noun "Martin" flashed into her mind, and she knew that was not correct. After a few moments, the voice spoke again.

"The initial is 'F'," it said.

Miss Mercer declared afterward that she immediately realized the name of the priest was "Fortin," a paragram for "Martin."

"What does he want me to do with the apple?" she asked.

"He says he owes it to you and always wanted to give it to you; so here it is. He says it's too bad that this is all he can do about it."

After the meeting, Miss Mercer told me the following story:

When she was about four years old, she met one of the village priests, who spoke to her and said she was such a good little girl that "some day" he would give her a "great big apple." The child did not let him forget his promise, but whenever she would meet him, he either did not have the apple available or it was inconvenient to get one for her.

Always she would ask for "my apple," but he would laugh and say he would have it for her "next time." "Next

—74—

time" never came, even though she said she importuned him regularly for several years.

As for the other symbols, she said the black cow must have been one which had been given to her mother as a wedding present but which her father actively disliked. In fact, it was such a subject of controversy and of some mistreatment that finally it had to be sold.

Miss Mercer said she did not know of any gold comb, but that it might be among a few items of jewelry which her mother had expected to inherit but which had been taken by a relative.

All of this added up to a fine collector's item, except—

It had been Miss Mercer's first encounter with mediumship. While in the beginning she said she was impressed by what had occurred, she began in our subsequent discussion to search for flaws in the test. She asked questions which produced more questions, and the answers were not always to her liking or contrary to her preconceptions. Limited by time and also by my inability to put satisfactory answers into words, our discussion tended to become argumentative, rather than clarifying. She, therefore, chose to end the matter permanently, so far as we were concerned, thus:

Her story of the meaning of the symbols, she confessed, was untrue. Her tale of the red apple, the black cow and the converted jewelry was a fabrication in its entirety. She had made it all up, she averred, merely to test my gullibility!

I gave her credit for an exceedingly clever and detailed imagination, and there the matter stood until about eight years later, in 1946. Miss Mercer was a guest for dinner in our home when my wife mentioned casually that I was working on a fictionized story about the after-life. Miss

Mercer recalled her visit to the Zenor class and, for the benefit of my wife, recounted in detail substantially the same things which were contained in her previous account, including the tale of the red apple, the significance of the black cow and the probable significance of the gold comb.

Moreover, she added one further detail which she had never revealed to me in the intervening years: Within a few weeks after the date of the meeting, the symbology of the casket was confirmed, for an uncle—a brother of her mother—had died. He was not considered a very close relative, as far as Miss Mercer was concerned, and as predicted, his death had no effect upon her life.

Upon being reminded of her earlier recantation, she at first could not remember that she had used such a device to terminate our 1938 discussion. When she did recall, she said she had found my arguments so persuasive but still so contrary to traditional opinions that she had decided to finish off the proof with one mortal blow.

On the other hand, the mere knowledge that communication is possible or its acceptance as a fact does not necessarily mean that the person convinced immediately becomes a better individual. It should stimulate a broader outlook, which in turn should bring about a fervent search for answers to the eternal "why" of life's mysteries. Finally this should bring about a higher moral standard, based upon a practical understanding of harmonious living. Unfortunately, such is not necessarily the case. What we know intellectually very often is merely the attractive object of our thinking, rather than an integral factor or motivator of our being—and that is liable to apply to the greatest, as well as the least, of us.

Intellectual recognition can be a valuable first step, but

it carries with it no guarantee of better conduct, as witness this experience:

Ben E. had become acquainted in 1946 with a young veteran of the Pacific war and, in fact, had befriended him by providing him with a place to live temporarily in overcrowded Los Angeles. A close friend of the veteran had been killed during the Battle of Okinawa, and so Ben suggested that a visit to one of Richard Zenor's meetings might prove that the friend was not really dead, after all. The veteran (we will call him Bill) said he did not believe in "that sort of thing" but agreed to go.

During the message period at the meeting, Ben first talked to someone, and then a voice through the medium interrupted:

VOICE (excitedly): This is Don, Bill! I'm not dead! I'm not dead! I'm all right. I don't know much about this stuff, but I'm learning, because I'm going to school. Remember how my nose used to itch?

BILL: Yeah.

VOICE: Well, it still does over here! Remember my teeth? Well, I have all my teeth now. Bill, you're going to be a success, and I'll be able to help you.

BILL: Did you die hard?

VOICE: Yes, but it was worth it.

At this time there were some signs of great emotion, almost to the point of tears, but no tears were actually shed by the medium. However, the contact was broken.

On the way out of the meeting, Bill said to Ben, "Well, that was him; it sounded just like him." Don often had complained of a peculiar tickling of the nose, he explained, and as for the teeth: "I knocked three of Don's teeth out, but it was like every fight we ever had—we were better friends than ever."

Convinced, then, that he had actually established communication with the world of the hereafter, the youthful veteran nevertheless was not sufficiently inspired to explore the significance of the test further. Instead, he disappeared from Ben's home a short time later without warning, and while there was no direct evidence of a connection, Ben said that he found that several important items of personal property had disappeared, too.

HELPERS, TONGUES AND SKEPTICS

VI

Wherefore tongues are for a sign, not to them that believe, but to them that believe not. . . .

—I Corinthians XIV: 22

THE TEACHERS who broadcast through Richard Zenor's radio-like telephone say that no soul is ever lost forever, but that many are temporarily lost in the darkness of their own ignorance and damned by the purgatorial confusions of the mental state they were in when they made the transfer to the astral world. Helpers, guides, teachers and celestial "angels" try to pierce the black or gray fog of their mental atmosphere and inspire them to attain a consciousness which will eliminate their distress and misery, but this is not always easy nor immediately possible. The encrustations of misunderstanding, disbelief and wrong thinking become so crystallized within the dark atmosphere that many years of suffering may be required before the soul breaks through this erroneous objective barrier and places the individual in a position to receive light and help.

Occasionally an individual who is confused and literally

"lost" in the lower regions of the other world may be quickly helped—i.e., "saved"—by temporarily restoring him to the objective environment of the earth plane. He is allowed to speak through the medium and, feeling himself in possession of a physical body in what, to him, is a normal atmosphere, his own mental state may be cleared just sufficiently to permit the helpers on the other side to reach him after he is again released from the physical shell. Those guarding the medium must exercise great care, however, to prevent any upset or emotional disturbance which would permanently impair the instrument. Nevertheless, the treatment does sometimes work.

A radio executive tells of this experience:

Through Richard Zenor, a voice spoke to him, giving the name of a man whom the executive had once befriended at a time when the friend was "down and out." The friend had died, and it was now three days after the date of cremation. The medium's hand tightly grasped that of the radio man, as though clutching at something substantial and familiar, and the voice cried out:

"Where am I? I'm not dead. What is this?"

The excitement broke the contact, but a week later the same voice spoke and in much the same way, adding:

"What the hell is this all about? Where am I?"

The executive attempted to explain as best he could, and finally the contact was broken.

The next week the voice came in singing, "Sailing, sailing, over the bounding main!" and then spoke with a new tone:

"I'm so happy. I'll never forget all you've done for me."

The personality gave thanks for receiving help from his friend in both worlds and concluded by saying he had been placed in a "rest home" in the astral world. He had, in fact, been "saved"!

Help for those willing to be helped extends through the two worlds in many other ways. It ranges from mental healing to guidance toward right action, often without the individual helped being objectively conscious of the help. The extent of the help and its efficacy all depend upon the mental attitude, as well as the destiny pattern, of the person for whom the help is intended, say the Zenor teachers.

Because the nature of spiritual help is as varied and divergent as the patterns of the universe itself, only now and then do we become aware of its dramatic import. In 1937 a singer, who was a regular attendant at one of the Zenor classes, was appearing in a Hollywood movie. On the set she met an actress-friend, Irma, who finally confessed that something was worrying her. She wondered if she were having hallucinations because she was approaching middle age (actually, she was only 39) and asked if she appeared to be acting strangely. She said that on three separate nights she had been awakened by a voice, which seemed to call repeatedly: "Irma! Irma! This is Carol!"

Twice she awakened her husband to tell him about the voice, but with pragmatic disregard for the mystic qualities of living he simply told her she was crazy. (How many psychiatrists, who list the hearing of voices as a delusion, would do the same?) She even imagined she heard the voice in the daytime when all was quiet.

The singer tried to persuade her to visit Richard Zenor, but Irma refused at first; she said she had never known anyone named "Carol" anyway. Induced by a ruse to visit with the medium, Irma heard various ones speak to her friend, the singer, and then a feminine voice burst through.

"Oh, Irma, I've had such a time getting to you!" it exclaimed.

In her lifetime, said·the voice, she had been a singer, and she gave her first name as "Carol." She explained that she had been attracted to Irma and wished to help her, but could do so more effectively if Irma were conscious of her presence and cooperation in the work they would do together.

The medium, of course, had been told nothing concerning the previous "hallucinations."

The same singer tells of another similar experience with a friend whose father-in-law had been deceased for some time. One night she awakened to hear his voice calling to her, apparently from outside the house.

"Pearl, Pearl, get up and look at the baby!" the voice seemed to urge.

In her drowsy state, Pearl forgot momentarily that her father-in-law was gone, and so aroused her husband to tell him:

"Your Dad's outside the window, calling to me."

As is usual, she was informed that she was "hearing things" and, when she wanted to investigate, her husband said, "Don't be foolish!" However, she did check on the baby—and found the child had turned around in its crib so that its head was where its feet should have been. Further movement could have caused a blanket to be twisted about the infant's face and head in such a way that there was danger of suffocation.

On the following day, Pearl related the experience to her friend, the singer, and as a result they decided to visit

Richard Zenor. One of the first to come through the instrument solved the mystery:

"This is Pop H——. My, what a time I had getting you up last night!"

After some conversation about the baby (of whom the father-in-law had been very proud), the voice remarked:

"I'm having a fine time over here. I haven't changed a bit. But, you know, I haven't heard a real good story since I've been over here!"

Pearl subsequently revealed that she had been in the habit of collecting jokes and anecdotes for her husband's father. (It should be noted, however, that the father-in-law's statement does not imply there is not a great deal of reminiscing and even joke-telling by many in the afterlife.)

The ability of balanced and intelligent persons to "hear voices" or to have other extra-sensory experiences is perfectly normal and, in fact, were we not so engrossed in the superficialities of our material existence, the development of psychic gifts would be the rule, rather than the exception. The teachers through Richard Zenor have often made this statement and have emphasized that all must eventually come to the realization that their perceptive powers are not limited to their five senses, a fact which is finally becoming well-established through the work of Dr. J. B. Rhine at Duke University and others in the field of parapsychology.

In general, our "sixth sense" and psychic faculties have been suppressed and dimmed by the encrustations of material experience, but every now and then we have proof that they do still exist. I recall one Zenor class meeting many years ago when each of us was asked to test our psychic abilities by exchanging an object, such as a ring or other piece of jewelry, with another member of the class. These objects, having been close to our persons for a relatively long time, were supposed to have taken on some of the "vibrations" or vibratory pattern of our auras. Held in front of the forehead, the "vibrations" would stimulate the pineal gland, we were told. This "all-seeing eye," as it is termed by some occultists, could pick up the tiny impulses, relay them to the brain, where they would be interpreted as mental pictures, something in the same way as vibratory patterns transmitted by radio are interpreted in the form of moving pictures by a television receiver.

Some in the class had a greater ability to receive and describe the pictures than others. My notes show that, after I handed my watch to a young woman class member, she described an automobile accident involving a coupe and a sedan. She later said she had never seen my car, and I had reason to believe this was correct, but she picked it out of a line of parked automobiles (there was a large number of cars parked in the vicinity, including several which were similar in appearance to mine) and said that it was the coupe which she had seen in her mental picture. A short time later, the machine was involved in a minor accident, but it was much less severe than the one which had been described. Perhaps I was more cautious, due to the warning. Or was it because my mind had become more acutely attuned, so I could receive substantial help from the other world in an emergency?

There is some objective evidence that spirit helpers do accompany the individual from place to place, watching his activities closely enough to make possible a later report. For instance, a "guide" or guardian, said to have been associated with me, once described in detail my efforts in trying to aid a young couple having legal difficulties. The guide complimented me for what I had done—or attempted to do, because an attempt to effect a reconciliation during a divorce proceeding had failed—and spoke quaintly of "that big white building, all about law," where the matter had occurred.

At other times, I attended meetings conducted by other mediums and then, through Richard Zenor, was told all about what had gone on, including references to particular conversations. In September, 1937, I attended a demonstration in Beverly Hills, at which Pat Marquis, the "boy with the X-ray eyes," read cards and printed pages, imitated gestures of the guests and moved easily about the room, although his eyes were carefully bandaged with heavy electrical tape. Among the guests was the late famed Judge Ben Lindsey, whom I knew quite well. During the evening we talked about the demonstration, and a few days later, one of the speakers through Richard Zenor not only referred casually to what had gone on, but repeated accurately part of the conversation I had had with Judge Lindsey out of the presence of all others at the demonstration. The communicator mentioned at first merely that the conversation had been with "a man," but added significantly, "I believe I heard you call him 'judge.' "

Incidentally, I observed with interest—in connection with previous statements as to the function of the pineal gland—that young Pat's ability to see in spite of his bandages was immediately frustrated if some metal object were held in front of his forehead; that is, in front of the gland. Physiologists have noted that in certain reptiles the gland has the structure of a physical eye and is called the "pineal eye."

While it might be objected that the purported observations of guides and helpers away from the presence of the medium could be accounted for on the theory of clairvoyance or "mind reading" by Richard Zenor himself, this would not explain evidences of spiritual help completely apart from the medium. For example, Mrs. R. was attempting to find a suitable apartment for herself in Los Angeles (in the days when suitable apartments were available). She said she seemed to be guided to one which turned out to be ideal, except for the price. It was more expensive than her budget would allow, but as she was discussing the matter with the owner, a woman, the latter suddenly said:

"Something tells me to rent this apartment to you."

Whereupon the rental was reduced to an amount acceptable to the prospective tenant.

No part of the transaction had anything to do with Richard Zenor's mediumship, except that Mrs. R., a class student, had been taught that she would always receive help whenever she needed it and to the extent that conditions—including the state of her own consciousness—would permit. A spirit friend, speaking through the instrument, told her later, "I just took you by the ear and led you there" (to the apartment).

In another case, the help operated directly through the medium. A man had been killed suddenly in an accident. His grieving wife finally was induced to go to a Zenor meeting, and she reported afterward she was satisfied that it was her husband who had talked with her. So certain was she, in fact, that she prevailed upon Mr. Zenor (and I use the word "prevailed" advisedly, because his private work is generally limited to regular students interested in spiritual unfoldment) to allow her to come back the following day. She arrived with a brief case and was with the medium for one and one-half hours. Afterward, she said her husband had helped her through a mass of business complications and legal papers, and she was able to clear up many matters pertaining to his estate.

Such testimony is interesting for its intimations of the manner in which discarnate personalities at times are able to assist those still struggling with the problems of the physical plane, but it is ordinarily not accepted as conclusive evidence by psychic researchers attempting to prove survival.

The well known phenomena of "polyglot mediumship," however, fit the requirements of acceptable proof more perfectly; that is, the proof is relevant to the case for survival and the credibility of the communicators through such an instrument as Richard Zenor. In his case, presumed spirit entities seem to have little or no difficulty expressing themselves in foreign languages. Considering the problems of control—since, after all, the instrument is an animate rather than a strictly mechanical telephone—the results have been highly satisfying.

A particularly clear channel is required to permit the accurate reproduction of a foreign tongue by vocal cords and a sound box, to say nothing of a conditioned nervous system, long used to only one language. Some observers have a tendency to discredit entirely the authenticity of a communication in a foreign language if the accent and idiom are at all tinged with the personality and language traits of the medium. Yet this may not necessarily invalidate the communication. It may simply be that the communicator is so immersed in the personality and speech pattern of the medium that the influence is inescapable.

Assuming that an animal could be a medium, for example, one can imagine the strange sounds which a human entity would make in trying to use the animal as an instrument of communication. This is an extreme assumption, of course, but illustrative of the problem of control through an aura of fixed habits and personality.

Where deviations from the known personality traits and speech habits of the manifesting entity are observed, the communication, therefore, need not be discredited without weighing the content of the message and other elements which might tend to prove authenticity. All mediums, I believe, are subject to this problem of personality interference to a greater or lesser degree, and misunderstanding of the nature of the problem leads many times to unjust denunciation. I would find it not at all unreasonable to accept as authentic a communication in English which was colored by the foreign accent of a trance medium having a different native language, provided other factors proved evidential.

However, these difficulties have been reduced to a minimum in the mediumship of Richard Zenor. His "deep trance" state during the full time of his communication sessions apparently clears the channel for many of the message-givers, whether they speak in a foreign language or not; his own personality usually impinges but little upon the over-shadowing communicator. As a result, many persons have reported receiving messages, not only in foreign languages, but correctly spoken, correctly accented and characteristically personalized in the particular foreign language.

Mr. S. Arion Lewis Jr., attorney for the Agasha Temple church corporation, once stated under oath that he had been able to recognize four or five foreign languages spoken through the medium, including Latin. He said he was not a linguist, but had sufficient knowledge of the languages identified to recognize them. I have personally convinced myself far beyond "a reasonable doubt" that Richard Zenor himself, as himself, speaks no other language than English. In the first place, the record of his activities since the age of four would permit him no time to perfect so remarkable a skill. Newspaper stories of his public appearances when he was very small report the same kind of language phenomena which have been observed continuously throughout the years. Secondly, an acquired skill would hardly include the ancient languages which have been recognized, or difficult living tongues, such as Hindustani, Polish, Russian, Chinese, Japanese and Hungarian.

Some years ago I made an imperfect recording of a child's voice as it came through the instrument. Some of the words and singing were indistinguishable because of the poor quality of the record, but upon playing it back for a language teacher whose native tongue was Spanish I was told that the distinguishable foreign words were certainly Spanish and that, more important, the accent, manner of speaking and personality of the little girl's voice calling itself "Maria" were typical and authentic. In fact, the teacher stated that it would be impossible for an English speaking person of Richard Zenor's background to imitate so perfectly the accent and speech mannerisms of this very feminine child's voice, even when the child was speaking English with a Mexican-Spanish accent, as she did several times during the recording. When I convinced the teacher that the voice had come through the lips and vocal cords of an adult man, she was astonished beyond words.

The radio executive mentioned previously told me that he had recognized as authentic Swedish a song that had been sung by one of the communicators, while another man reported that he had talked to his father in Dutch. In this last case, the father additionally proved his identity by reminding his son of an incident that occurred in Holland and was known only to the two of them. There was still another bit of evidence for the son: Controlling the medium's body, the father had patted his son on the back in a typically Dutch fashion.

"It was never an embrace—always a pat on the back— when my father was alive; so I was sure it really was my father," said the son.

These reports of characteristic gestures, incidentally, have become almost commonplace. The medium's arm or leg will be thrust out and moved around, and the communicator will say, "See, I can walk now!"; or, "Look, there is nothing wrong with my arm now!"

In one instance, a young woman attended a message meeting for the first time and was surprised when the medium's hand moved to her neck and found a hidden chain, which was gradually drawn out to reveal a tiny charm on the end. This charm had great significance for her, she said, because it had been given to her by her fiance before his death. She was certain that it was he who came to her, since he reminded her of the words he had spoken when he gave her the trinket.

The almost prosaic, unflamboyant method of presenting the communications, without props or theatrical trappings, conceals on occasion a dramatic content not readily appreciated by all witnesses. Following is the report of a message in which a foreign language and an unusual gesture served to convince a skeptic:

Miss R. had already talked on previous occasions with her father through the instrument in Spanish and wanted her doubting sister to have the same experience. First, Miss R. spoke to a feminine voice she said was that of a friend in the other world named Mila. The conversation then changed.

MILA: *Te quiere hablar tu papá.* (Your father wishes to speak to you.) (Note the singular form of the Spanish "you.")

MISS R.: *¿Es mi papá, Mila?* (Is it my father, Mila?)

MILA (indicating the sister): *No, es el papá de ella.* (No, it is her father.)

SISTER (nonplussed): *¿Quién es?* (Who is it?)

MALE VOICE: *Manuelito.*

SISTER (recognizing the affectionate form of the name of her late father-in-law): *¿Cómo estás?* (How are you?)

VOICE: *No muy bien.* (Not very well.) (The father-in-law had died as the result of a serious illness less than three months previously. Note that physical conditions brought over from the earth world into the new life often hang on until the individual learns to clear his mental atmosphere.)

VOICE (continuing): *Hija, voy a estar con Vds. para ayudarles. No tengas cuidado. Todo va a salir bien.* (Daughter, I am going to be with you all to help you. Do not worry. Everything will come out all right.) (There had been distressing illnesses in the sister's family.)

VOICE (continuing, as the medium's hands moved to his face and began patting his own cheeks): *Acaríciame la cara, Amelita.* (Pat my face, Amelita.)

MISS R. (in English): What is the matter with that man's face?

SISTER: Nothing; he just wants me to pat it.

The contact was then broken. As soon as she could, the sister explained. In 1944, she and her husband had visited the home of his father, Manuel, in Puebla, Mexico. Between the daughter-in-law and Manuel there had sprung up a little joke. Manuel's own daughters, when greeting him, were in the habit of patting his cheeks affectionately with both their hands. He jokingly asked his daughter-in-law why she did not do the same, but she teasingly refused each time he asked, and there was considerable banter on both sides as a result. The matter was quickly forgotten—until the night she got a telephone call from another world. She was convinced, she said, that the connection had been completed. Furthermore, Miss R. knew nothing of the incident, and no member of her family was in the habit of calling the sister "Amelita" . . . no one except Manuel.

Sometimes the "speaking in tongues" is dramatic even when the receiver cannot understand the tongue. A Chinese attempted to speak to a visitor, who unfortunately did not understand. However, someone who understood Mandarin, the form of Chinese being spoken, was able to translate and to pass on some useful information.

A similar situation arose at a message service in 1943 when two young women were addressed by a voice speaking Polish. Again a translator (the same linguist as above) was able to help. The manifesting entity claimed to be their grandfather and, in Polish, told them a number of facts about their family. The girls thereafter admitted they

—92—

were of Polish descent, but that they were able to understand only a few words of the language.

Still more dramatic is this true story told to me by a noted author and lecturer, who has investigated the instrumentality of Richard Zenor:

During the war, he mentioned his interest to an actress friend, who, though an avowed skeptic, insisted that he take her to one of the meetings. After the author had received a message, a feminine voice began speaking to the actress in Hungarian, for she originally was from Budapest. At first she did not respond; so the author asked her if she understood. She said she did.

"Then why don't you speak to her?" whispered the author.

The actress began to weep, but whispered back: "She says she is my mother—and she can't be."

Nevertheless, the actress and the voice carried on an extended conversation in Hungarian. But once away from the meeting the young woman began to "storm" at the author. ("Storm" is his word.) The medium was a fraud, she said. It was impossible, horrible. . . . Her mother was not dead. The things the voice told her could not be true. How could she be expected to believe it was her mother, who was alive in Hungary? So emotional was her tirade that the author felt obliged to remind her that he had not asked her to attend the meeting; that she had insisted on going. And the voice did speak Hungarian, did it not? She admitted this was true, but still maintained that some monstrous fraud had been committed.

Practically a whole year passed before there was a tragic confirmation of this unbelieved telephone call from another world. The actress had been away from her family for some time; the war interrupted their letters. Then one day there was a letter. Well before the time of the "call" through Richard Zenor, the mother and several other members of her family in Hungary had died as the direct result of war privations—just as the voice had said. The communicator had only wanted the daughter to know that they had found peace . . . in a world without war.

Yet the message would not necessarily have been invalidated had it developed that the mother was still in her physical body at the time of the communication. What about the many reported cases we have mentioned in which persons pronounced dead or under anaesthesia (or in some other super-normal state) have reported, upon reviving, that they found themselves detached from their body and were even able to view what was going on about it? Though still attached to its own physical shell, should we not expect such displaced entities to manifest occasionally through the physical shell of a receptive medium? The answer, of course, is that this very thing has happened. My notes based on an incident in 1936 illustrate:

Mr. B. attended a meeting at which his deceased brother talked and convincingly identified himself. Then another voice spoke—spoke with a peculiar clipped speech that was very familiar.

"Bertie, what's going on here? What are you doing here?" demanded the voice.

Mr. B., whose first given name is Willis, had not been called "Bertie" or "Bert" (his middle name) for 20 years; so he asked who was talking.

"Don't you know who this is? It's Bill, your brother," insisted the voice.

"But you're not dead!" exclaimed Mr. B.

"No, I'm still up in the hospital at Hot Springs. But

it's lonesome up there. Write me, damn you, write me!"

Mr. B. explained he had written, but the voice replied that the letters were not received. (A later checkup disclosed that the letters had gone astray.) When the voice was asked how it happened to be coming through the medium, the reply was:

"Well, they told me to get in here and talk, and that's what I did. I don't know where I am, but I can see you all right. Can you see me?"

"No, I can't see you, but I can hear you very well," Mr. B. replied.

The conversation ended with Mr. B's promise to visit the brother in the Hot Springs, S. D., hospital where he was being treated. After the meeting, Mr. B. checked by telegraph to make sure his brother was still alive—which he was, and still is at the time of this writing. Mr. B. also learned that the brother had undergone surgery on the day before the Zenor meeting.

Subsequently the brother confirmed that he did have some kind of strange experience on the day following the operation, but for some reason refused to discuss it.

WHO ARE THE TEACHERS?

VII

INTERSPERSED WITH ALL the message-giving, which is the strictly telephonic phase of Richard Zenor's mediumship, there is the constant reminder that a deeper significance lies behind such an important connection with the other world. In fact, the messages are but a kind of lure to arouse the objective interest and so permit the inherent soul-interest to manifest itself. Then will commence the individual's unfoldment and his realization of bounds beyond his limited earth world; then will begin the true search for the meaning of his Odyssey.

Once the intellectual sense has become assured of the reliability of the instrument, the questions are likely to begin to flow: What is the other world like? What is the activity there? Is it a place or a state? Where do we actually go from here? Is "heaven" only a name, or is it a place, too? And what about the "other place"? When we leave this world, do we ever return? What is the meaning of all our trouble on earth? What is the meaning of life?

There is no end to the questions, nor is there, apparently, any final, exhaustively complete answer to them in this life. But in a language ill-adapted to the expression of abstract truths, made up, as it is, of the symbols of our materiality, those who seem to know some of the answers try to pass their wisdom on to us in the best way they can.

Some are individuals with little more experience than you and I. Others are more advanced, and they come back as preliminary teachers to coach us out of our kindergarten habits. Among the message-givers, probably the commonest report they give us is that they are "going to school" or attending classes in the other world. So they remind us that it is well we begin to consider our preliminary lessons here.

The mediumship of Richard Zenor is particularly significant because it has become possible for this instrument to be used as a channel by teachers of an unusually high order—Master Teachers as they are sometimes called.

Who, then, are these Master Teachers, long talked about by so many and understood by so few?

Are they the angels and archangels of the Bible? Are they the saints of the church? Or are they the mahatmas of India and the gurus who guide their disciples along a mystic path toward enlightenment? Or are they like the Greek heroes who have become demi-gods, wise in the ways of gods and men?

Then again, are they magicians and master alchemists, capable of transmuting the base metal of ignorance into the gold of understanding? Or are they the builders of the pyramids and the master masons of the secret temples of initiation?

Are they the initiates of the ancient mysteries, surviving in their tradition but teaching in new ways through modern channels the arcana of the ages?

Or are they the simple, humble men of all time who have glimpsed the face of Isis through the thinner veils of inner truth and by charity and compassion, through peace and meditation and by humility and simplicity have become the arisen ones who point the way to the place prepared for men of accomplished virtue?

Like religions which are apart but together in their separateness, the Master Teachers can be said to be all of these things and more. They are not duplicates of each other, clothed in the sameness of a higher light, but as various as the infinite facets of their enlightenment and only as same as their light is a reflection of and expression of a single, total source. That is what they themselves tell us.

The whole subject of the Master Teachers is a perfectly practical matter. Those who have attended the classes of Richard Zenor in Los Angeles have been given some simple, satisfying explanations of their spiritual capabilities and origins without detracting from the dignity and transcendental quality of their advanced state. As Agasha, the principal teacher of the Zenor classes, puts it:

"Your teacher can do nothing for you that you cannot do for yourself."

The reason is plain, he says, when it is realized that the real master teacher of every individual is himself; that is:

"Your soul is your greatest teacher, and all the efforts of any outside teacher are bent toward unfolding the wisdom of the soul and bringing it to your objective consciousness. In reality, your soul knows everything, for it is a part of the great universal God-consciousness. When you are ready, the master will appear—the master within you."

This does not mean that we do not receive help and inspiration of a substantial nature from individual teachers of a high order. Those whose consciousness is attuned to that order respond accordingly and are thereby vital-ized and stimulated to release within themselves those powers and that realization which seek objective expression in the world of material experience. One musician listening to the work of a master musician is inspired to release from within himself that which may be a new master work. The teacher may point the way and mark the pitfalls, may even prescribe techniques and educate the student by reciting the history and experience of others, but never, according to Agasha, may he substitute his actions for the responsibility of the student.

For the truth is that all the angels and all the mahatmas, all the masters and all the gurus, are but individuals like ourselves—like we are in our universal aspect and unlike us only to the extent that our unfoldment through solution of the problems of experience has left us here still encased in a darker aura of illusive separation from the Oneness of the universe.

Agasha emphasizes time and again that neither he nor any other Master Teacher (of whom there are thousands and thousands attempting to inspire and awaken the benighted souls of these "latter days") has reached a final state, a spiritual dead-end. Seemingly, there is always progress and progression. There is always a teacher on the path ahead to light the way for a willing disciple. Agasha still has his own teacher in the far-reaches of the mother of worlds he calls "Immensity," just as he in his turn seeks to urge up the Jacob's ladder of advancement those who are behind him.

The Master Teachers, then, are but men who have made good; who have perfected themselves through experience and understanding, even as each of us is perfected through unfoldment. They are masters only because they have completely acheived self-mastery. They are gods to the extent that we all are gods and sons of God; in the sense that all are irreplaceable extensions and incorporations of the one God-consciousness. Like the cell is a part of the god that is the individual, so all of us are joined together within the unfolding principle of life and consciousness with an interdependence and integrity of purpose that provides each of us with the potentialities of mastership.

This is the teaching of Agasha and an abridged summation of the teachings of all true masters. It is neither apart from nor entirely a part of the physical expressions of the universe. And the angels and teachers are not so much the administrators as the interpreters or translators of the law, stating and restating it in terms of our own experience, so that we may bring into focus our own understanding in the light of universal principles.

Not, as we have said, that there is no protection or tangible help from these teachers, as well as from many lesser guides. There are seven associated solar systems, of which ours is one, says Agasha, and there are seven associated Master Teachers who spread their benevolent regency, their light and their understanding to the myriad teachers of all these systems in order that we may all remain "on the path."

But always the extent to which we may be helped is conditioned by the breadth of our understanding or, more correctly, our realization. We begin to realize objectively what our souls intuitively already know. The lessons of experience become easier, and understanding is accelerated when pure realization substitutes for the harder lessons of trial and error. It is the teacher's function to promote realization to the full extent of our consciousness, and with it comes assistance of a personal and concrete nature, according to all we have learned by our development.

Thus do we prove the rule that the God-consciousness helps us most when we help ourselves, by an understanding self-reliance. We thereby attract to ourselves what will also objectively be of help to ourselves and those about us.

No man can escape himself, says Agasha; no man can escape his responsibility to himself—to release that which is within himself, namely, an unfolding expression of the whole. No teacher can substitute his wisdom for that which comes through individual understanding, but there will be great teachers, even in this age and in the flesh, who will inspire within men the realization of their spiritual destiny and inseparableness from each other and the universal whole.

We are in the "latter days" of darkness before light, say the Master Teachers, the last days of rampant evil born of ignorance and self-repression before the dawn of a Golden Age. But while we wait for this long-promised age of peace, enlightenment, of material advancement and general prosperity, such things as these will be added unto us only according to the degree that our consciousness and our conscience break through the mists of misunderstanding and search out the veiled truths which are really searching us out by seeking expression through us.

Meanwhile, the Master Teachers voice a warning: This, too, is the era of false teachers and faulty prophets. Nor is it a time when all who purport to communicate from the spirit worlds are messengers of wisdom. As a test, the higher teachers propose: Beware the "teacher" who promises to give that which has not been earned, the "something for nothing" that attracts us all. There are those in the lower levels of the super-physical realms who interpret the law according to their wishes and their frustrations, rather than their knowledge, even as they did on earth. Because of their accumulated encrustations of prejudice and ignorance, they can no more easily communicate with the universal Master Teachers than can the equally ignorant earth-bound beings they have left behind on this plane.

There are no arbitrary dictators among the higher teachers. The messenger or the instructor who is authentic, the guide or helper who is sincere will not arbitrarily substitute his will for that of the student but will seek to guide and inspire the physically bound individual to a full realization of his own powers and opportunities which he has earned. As has been taught by the initiates of all times, no man can be greater than he is—according to the development of his consciousness—but often he is less than he can be, both in his aspirations and his accomplishments.

Many who have regularly attended services and classes at Rev. Richard Zenor's Agasha Temple of Wisdom in Los Angeles have received inspiration and instruction apart from the group lectures. Inspirational messages often take the form of short discourses during times when the student is able to converse directly with the manifesting voices. Throughout these messages runs the theme of help from the spiritual spheres, combined with self-help —the theme that material conditions are neither to be ignored nor merely tolerated but are susceptible of improvement as their meaning in terms of learning a lesson and understanding life becomes absorbed into the expanding consciousness of the individual.

Here is a typical conversation:

VOICE: Good evening. I am very happy to be in a position to descend and speak unto you and give you my blessings.

WOMAN: I am glad to have you come.

VOICE: Do not fear. We know that the future holds better things for you, because I am helping you to work out that which will be good for you in this embodiment. I am doing everything I can to help you, and all will be given to you in a way you will like if you will but go on as you have. Those other folks are doing a little better now.

WOMAN: I think they are, too. I am so glad you are helping them.

VOICE: Yes, they are managing to do things that they are supposed to do at this time, according to their environment. There is not very much they can do under the circumstances, but there will be a better vibration coming for them, and I feel they are very sincere and know that God is with them and going to help them.

WOMAN: I know you have helped them.

VOICE: Indeed I do, and you will find that God will be good to them, because they have earned it in this life.

*   *   *

Another typical conversation:

VOICE: Good evening, my child.

WOMAN: Good evening.

VOICE: Well, you can see that we have accomplished much.

WOMAN: That is right, and I am grateful.

VOICE: I know you are grateful. If we live in the divine state, child, we will always accomplish the things we set forth to do, if we take the right attitude. Sometimes the difficulties we go through and the experiences we have merely come to us to help to build character. They help us to be strong. I think you know that, don't you?

WOMAN: That is right.

VOICE: I am very grateful to know that you have accomplished on the earth what you want to. We have much more to accomplish, and we will grow spiritually. Each night call upon me and call upon the higher state of consciousness, and you will receive power to help you on the path. God bless you.

The words of another teacher to a student are along the same line:

VOICE: Manifest into the true light, my child, and bring forth what you want; that is, as you earn it, every step of the way. Fear not and know that I am with you with a message given unto the world by the great teachers. The God-consciousness grows within. You know that. Once we recognize the higher self, then all things can come to us that are good for us on the earth plane. . . . As you go on, if you stay on the path, you will bring forth the spiritual light. God bless you, my child.

Such individual messages come from teachers and "guides" who have been attracted to the student in accordance with his rate of development. For the most part, however, the higher teachings, the statements of philosophy reminiscent of the profound wisdom taught in the ancient mystery schools, have been unfolded slowly and carefully in classes and public lectures over a long period of years. The speakers, in most cases, use the entranced medium as their instrument with a natural facility and humble dignity that is attractive to the average listener. By employing only simple expressions and avoiding highly technical vocabulary, they succeed also in holding the interest of audiences composed of many types of minds.

As we have noted, spiritual teachers need not necessarily be "graduates" who have permanently established themselves beyond all the earthly spheres. They may be souls with lesser development but, nevertheless, great understanding.

No doubt everyone has at some time heard of the illuminated ones known variously as adepts, initiates and masters. Some, like Jesus, have demonstrated their great wisdom while still in the physical body. More often, however, the Master Teachers have finally escaped—or, rather, graduated from—the so-called cycle of necessity which binds the vast majority of us to the wheel of material experience. Yet all such teachers whom we are able to contact attempt to guide mankind toward an illumined state and a full understanding of life.

If they cannot directly communicate their wisdom, they seek to inspire others in lower categories of consciousness, including the advanced earth souls, to act as beacons for those less advanced. Fortunately, from time to time the higher teachers have found it possible down through the ages to communicate directly with some individuals and groups, doing so for the purpose of keeping alive the wisdom teachings which are the keys to our existence and to our reason for being. The teacher called Agasha and the other high teachers associated with him are in this category.

Who is this Agasha?

What we know of him, of course, is based upon his

own words, and it is an interesting story. He tells us that in his last earthly life, some 7000 years ago, he was the religious and spiritual leader of a small section of population in what is now known as Egypt.

The Nile Valley and Delta were in a constant state of strife, due to religious, as well as political, differences. Wars among the small independent states were frequent, and doctrinal differences between the politico-religious systems of the various principalities were a constant source of irritation among the clannish populations of the communities.

Some of this clannishness and rivalry has survived even until now among the natives along the Nile south of the Delta. There, in many cases, it is virtually a disgrace to marry outside the village where one is born, and the clannishness of village society is evident in other ways. For example, archaeologists often prefer to employ men from a single village on important projects, rather than to attempt to mix recruits from two or more villages.

As the head of a small theocracy, much like others in the Nile Valley, Agasha perceived the uselessness and stupidity of the constant strife. He, therefore, took the lead in forming a kind of Egyptian United Nations of its day, finally bringing together 37 formerly independent governments into a single federation. Each of these governments, it must be understood, had represented a different religious sect, and consequently their drawing together meant development of a single religious or philosophical system, with erstwhile distinctions as to doctrine and understanding of universal principles completely resolved. Thereafter, for several hundred years the federation preserved a state of peace and harmony of an order which, up to then, was unknown in the land.

The priest-kings of the federation united their beliefs in a religious concept that embraced recognition of a universal spirit and the equality of individual opportunity to advance through self-development and self-unfoldment toward perfect harmony with that spirit. So the teachings of the principles of spiritual growth, as well as communication with advanced personalities in the spirit world, went on for a considerable period.

Agasha was the acknowledged leader of this new and broader theocracy, and through him contact was made with his spiritual teacher, then no longer in the body, for the purpose of receiving instruction concerning the higher planes of the spirit world and the meaning of the earthly existence in relation to the after-earth life. According to Agasha, the united leaders of the once rival sects became the initiates who today return through the instrumentality of Richard Zenor to instruct modern seekers after wisdom.

Their spiritual instructors, says Agasha, included the great arisen initiate called Amon, whose worship as a god became so prevalent during the later corruption of his philosophy in Egypt. Likewise associated with this group, according to Agasha's story, was one called Krai-o (a purely phonetic spelling, as is the case with most Asiatic and ancient names). It was Krai-o, says Agasha, who returned to Palestine and Egypt some 5000 years later for the completion of his own earth cycle as Jesus, the great Master Teacher, whose philosophy has so often been compared to the ancient wisdom religions of Egypt and the Far East.

So far, there is little of the Agashan story which can be verified from physical records, but he has promised that in the comparatively near future records will be unearthed which will give details of the unification of the sects in

Egypt and his part in that program. He has further stated that a large plaque, a symbol of the united 37 sects, with a central pyramidal design, will also be found not far from Cairo and not so very far from the three principal pyramids of Egypt.

As an interesting sidelight, Agasha has also announced that a wealthy and influential Egyptian, who was his son at the time of the unification of the sects, will have a leading part in excavation work planned by archaeologists. Many rich finds are promised, including ornaments and objects of great value and ancient records which long were believed lost with the destruction of the great Alexandrian library. He says, in fact, that evidences of a highly developed civilization will be found in the Nile Valley, exceeding in wealth and material advancement the later, more recent cultures with which we are now more familiar. Linkages between this virtually pre-historic civilization and a great culture that preceded the Deluge, or the sinking of the so-called lost continent of Atlantis, will also be discovered, Agasha has declared.

All of these statements, predictions and bits of history are stripped of their fantastic implications and are presented with matter-of-fact simplicity by the teachers when speaking through Richard Zenor. There has been so much of what they have said that interlaces into a fine pattern of logic, reason and a practical way of life, and so much of what they have predicted has already come to pass in our own fantastically changing world that longtime observers of the manifestations cannot but honor them at their face value, without serious doubts and with a desire to learn and understand more.

To that end, the teachers try to answer questions, both mental and audible, in an attempt to resolve the admittedly "intricate" (their word) problems of universal living. That the difficulties of transmitting information which will inspire understanding are great is reiterated frequently, especially the difficulty of expressing these matters in a language which we will understand but which fundamentally is foreign to them.

For the teachers do not use the instrument in quite the same way as most spirit-entities who are able to talk fluently through it. We are told that each teacher in his or her own realm (and we must remember that the positive and negative, the male and female counterparts, are of equal importance in the Great Plan) has a "desire body," which is a perfected form preserving the best traits of individuality and personality that have been molded into the autonomous soul down through eons of development. But in making use of the physical mechanism of the medium, the teachers generally appear only as lights, being otherwise formless in physical terms on this plane.

Those in lower degrees or the "astral" plane of after-earth living describe how the presence of Agasha, for instance, will often become noticeable to them by the arrival of a great shaft of gold, blue or white light, which builds up in the room, flooding and stimulating all with its brilliant power. This then enters the physical shell of the medium, and the control is completed by utilizing not only the physical organs necessary for expression but likewise the mental patterns of the brain. Language difficulties are thus to some extent overcome, since the vocabulary resources of the medium are thereby made available to the teacher.

Nevertheless, anyone who has studied the speech of the medium and of the teachers must become aware very quickly that the latitude of expression available to the latter is far greater than the medium's own personal resources. In fact, it is evident that the teachers draw upon their listeners and from other sources for vocabulary to give expression to their ideas, and while the basic style is traceable to the medium's own mentality, the full capacity for expression extends much beyond his powers.

In my own experience, I have noted that these teachers have reached out into my mental atmosphere for words and phrases which are distinctively peculiar to my way of thinking. Yet I may not have uttered those expressions at all in the presence of the medium.

I recall an occasion when I visited a discussion group conducted by a brilliant psychologist, who reached certain philosophical conclusions on the basis of modern research. He said, however, that he found it necessary to devise a new "terminology" in order to express more succinctly the ideas which he wanted to get across.

At the next Zenor class, where I regularly took notes, the teacher Agasha began his lecture by stating that he was not interested in establishing a "new" system of philosophy but was desirous of presenting in the simplest way all that he felt could be grasped concerning the universal philosophy.

"I try to eliminate the complicated terms which are usually used by earthly teachers," he said. "I do not wish to coin words but to use the simplest terms possible in your language."

I have long observed that the expression of profound and transcendental ideas in the available language, the language of the listener, with recourse to a minimum of strange words or even names, has characterized the Agashan lectures since their beginning.

So it is that it becomes apparent we have only touched

upon the "intricacies" of our metnod of communication. These "Lights of the World" who animate the instrument have a beautiful simplicity, both in their appearance as lights and in their statement of the fundamental principles of their wisdom. But like the veils of Isis that ever hide other veils to tantalize one's desire for a full view of the face of truth, the explanations of the purpose and meaning of life always give rise to new questions and new searches for satisfying answers.

Were it not so, we would be, not here, but in the hereafter, our earthly lessons learned and the romance of our Odyssey reduced to a sterile contemplation of abstractions in a vacuum.

VIII

Behold, what manner of love the Father hath bestowed upon us, that we should be called the sons of God.

—I John III: 1

For as many as are led by the Spirit of God, they are the sons of God. . . . The Spirit itself beareth witness with our spirit, that we are the children of God.

—Romans VIII: 14, 16

IN THE COSMIC CONCEPTION of life, everything has meaning and nothing is without reason. All things are related to their causes, and no cause is without a purpose. Each spark of divine consciousness is growing toward a state of individual realization and personal responsibility, but all are within themselves a part of and expressions of the Great Mover of all things, the indescribable Motivator of Purpose, the Oneness of the material and the spiritual universe, the Universal Consciousness that men call God.

If we do not see meaning in this remote outpost of the God-consciousness, or if men say the meaning is not according to their logic, it is not because there is no meaning. It is merely that they are not yet in a position to perceive it. Such explanations as are offered in the crude, artificial language of their life are never satisfying, never complete, but neither do these explanations merit rejection on the ground of inadequacy. They can still stimulate the individual to bring about his own understanding in inexpressible terms from within. The inadequacy lies with the individual, not with ultimate truth. Truth is changeless and finally approachable only through the language of the soul and the expanding of an inextinguishable divine light that is a part of all.

Such is the essence of the Agashan approach to wisdom. There is nothing new about it, nothing different. Its attraction lies in the fact that it is not different, that it has the ring of undifferentiated truth. It is as old as eternity and as universal as religion iself. For Agasha emphasizes, not the differences between religions, but their similarities. All great philosophies are but facets or dim views of a single understanding. Where the dogmas now conflict, growth of understanding must ultimately bridge all differences and resolve all disputes.

There is only one true religion, says Agasha. And in the end that will be found to be a composite of all of the inspired religions, whose great teachers have in their way been attuned to the Universal Consciousness of Immensity. They have stated and restated their vision of the aspects of truth in their terms and as was best designed for the understanding of their times. The paradoxes have been only apparent; the fundamental morality the same. There is no new *way* to truth or salvation, no exclusive approach to Deity. The *Way* is old and the same; only the restatement is apparently different.

The keystone of the arch which marks the Agashan, the universal *Way* is individual responsibility and complete spiritual democracy within the plan of unchanging law. And as in physics, so throughout nature, the basic law is:

For every action, there is an equal and opposite reaction.

That is the Law of Compensation, the impersonal guiding force of matter and spirit, the karmic principle of self-education and self-knowledge. Its administrator is the soul itself, inseparable from the all-embracing divine soul of the universal God-consciousness, and its role in human destiny is measured by the conscious awakening of the individual to an objective realization of his place in the divine plan.

To understand perfectly the workings of the law is the goal of many lifetimes of experience and contemplation of the meaning of experience. The beginner in the kindergarten school of universal understanding must start by correcting some deep-rooted superstitions concerning his state of being in the next world.

First, his soul after leaving the physical body does not sleep without awakening until some distant Judgment Day. Every day is judgment day for every soul.

Second, he does not graduate from the earth plane to a state of eternal idleness, rest and bliss, nor to one of eternal damnation. Such states, if they occur at all, are encountered because of the consciousness of the individual and are never more than temporary interruptions of his unfoldment.

Third, he does not upon leaving his present body promptly become a master of all of the secrets of heaven and earth, capable of revealing the true answers to all problems and mysteries in either his world or ours. Actually in most cases he will be about as ignorant or as wise directly after his passing as he was before.

The state of consciousness which he attains in "heaven" or "hell" is entirely dependent upon his own personal state of consciousness, his own personal heaven or hell created within himself. He will be exactly the kind of individual in spirit that he was on earth, except that his mental faculties will predominate in creating or attracting his environment. But though he create for himself a veritable hell in which to burn out the black transgressions of his earthly personality, progress to a higher state is inevitable in time. Eventually the messengers of light will reach into the abyss and make their presence felt, inspiring him to rise to new levels of consciousness. As we have said, everyone gets what he deserves in the hereafter, because he himself has created the consciousness in which he must live until that consciousness is changed.

Still, no man is beyond hope or beyond redemption. Through his own efforts, he may at any time reform his consciousness and thereby attune himself to a higher light that will mitigate his afflictions. It is in this way that God truly helps those who help themselves. No one person or group is specially favored; nor does anyone have an exclusive approach to truth. The true *Way* is as variable as the individual, but the workings of the law favor no one over another.

In the beginning of our material cycle, we are told, we descended from the core of life through the perfect consciousness of Immensity into the imperfect and confusing wave patterns of earthiness, a consciousness which became conditioned by successive life waves in need of objective expression. At first, life hung suspended in the lower astral light, then finally completed the descent from the original heavenly home, the perfect "Garden of Eden," into the realm of matter. On this planet, as on others, the waves of life developed and evolved in the world of forms, seeking by this experience to fathom the divine plan.

In the Agashan lectures, as in the ancient philosophical systems heretofore recorded, such words as "self-expression," "self-realization," and "self-unfoldment" and "individualization" abound. Prior to the "fall" from the perfect paradise of which the divine lights or soul-sparks were a part, each potential ego, it seems, lacked the objective consciousness which the Universal Spirit, the totality called God, "deemed it necessary" (Agasha's words) to have. Hence, material expression through form, the "original sin," was undertaken. The descent from the Garden of Eden into matter was, in effect, a long, cyclic journey into a realm of shadows—shadows which were the imperfect reflections of the perfect consciousness inherent in each ego, each manifestation of the divine light. The shadows became the material forms, and so are the imperfect reflections of our true selves.

But because they are shadows, imperfect configurations in the divine harmony, they are not to be scorned, says Agasha, for they are the expression of the very purpose for which we exist in this world. They are the means toward objective realization—that is, a device whereby we may bring about individual self-consciousness ("self-expression," "self-realization") *by observing objectively the shadows of our true selves.* In no other way could we achieve self-awareness and individual God-consciousness.

We who are men and women in this age have come a long way along the road to self-realization. We have unfolded and evolved through myriad cycles of physical experience, according to Agasha, and we have long confused the shadows of reality with the true light. But by this long train of experience we will all eventually understand the divine purpose of life, both objectively, because of our observations of the shadows we throw off, and subjectively, as we have always known, by the inward and submerged consciousness that is the all-knowing (though heretofore undelineated) divine self.

While these concepts obviously are difficult to express in words which are themselves but the products of shadows, Agasha in simple terms makes it clear that the purpose of life is not merely to be good and to do good but that good living, full living is a means to an end: The goal is to discover the pattern of life and the individual's relationship to it. This is accomplished through "self-expression," the process of studying one's reflections in the forms of material experience, leading finally to "self-realization," the objective awareness of self in relation to other "selves" and the great all-embracing Divine Self. And the process can be just as painless as the individual chooses it to be, according to his understanding of the law and the use of his "free will."

Faith, without questioning and without works, is not enough. The goal must be understanding—wisdom— with supreme faith that we are inherently capable of understanding and that through a true appraisal of our good and bad works, of our imperfect expressions in the shadowland of materiality, we may be lead toward wisdom.

Hence, the apparently paradoxical statement—but it is only apparent—that *the purpose of life is to discover its purpose.* That is our *raison d'être,* our reason for being. Therefore, it is never sufficient merely to be and do good, but we strive to understand, through our experience with the shadows of truth which we can observe and create objectively, *why* goodness (another name for internal and external harmony) is imperative. We observe the shadows in order to observe ourselves by seeing our reflections, "darkly, as in a mirror."

A lack of goodness, then, is mainly a failure to understand the true nature of ourselves and the basic harmony of the universe, due to an improper interpretation of the meaning of the shadows. Through "self-unfoldment," which is the process of reflecting and finally expressing in the shadow world the true light within each of us, we harmonize the objective and subjective consciousness, understand the meaning of our experiences in the world of imperfections and after an ages-long Odyssey return finally to our permanent residence in the heavenly home we originally left. We have by then understood that our leaving and our journey were like any traveler's adventure—a method of experience and of learning with graduation to conscious wisdom as the just reward.

It is not necessary to examine all of the philosophical arguments regarding the responsibility for suffering and pain in a planned universe to understand the law of reactions; nor to engage in an extended discussion of free will vs. destiny. If we remember the Agashan axiom that all matter and form, the very worlds themselves, are basically expressions of consciousness, rather than ultimate realities apart from consciousness, the philosophical difficulties may not be so abstruse.

It is common practice among the communicators to speak of locations in the spirit world and on the earth plane as states of consciousness; i.e., the "consciousness of Los Angeles," or the "astral consciousness," the "consciousness of Immensity," etc. There is good reason for this, because, as we have tried to emphasize, all these worlds of form are but outward, shadowy expressions of our individual and group consciousness in process of unfoldment. This ancient concept is no longer considered fantastic, even in the field of physical science, where leading thinkers long since have abandoned mechanism as a valid explanation of the laws of the universe and have gone so far as to describe matter itself as only a mental concept. (In the Agashan interpretation, matter is something more than a mere concept, something less than ultimate reality; it may be said to be a utilitarian extension of consciousness—the useful textbook of our first lessons in understanding ourselves.)

Furthermore, science now conceives of a finite, closed universe, in which even the total number of atoms and electrons may be computed. It is said that, if one atom were lost, the universe would fall, which is tantalizingly reminiscent of the Biblical reminder that even the hairs of our head are all numbered and one sparrow "shall not fall on the ground without your Father." Matter is pictured by science as a complex of waves and vibrations in an indefinable ether. All is found to be completely interrelated and so mutually interdependent that a change in any part must theoretically concern the whole.

The action and reaction of the etheric forces (a term used for want of a better one), consequently, becomes intimately involved with the processes of consciousness. The shadows of consciousness, which range themselves into the patterns of relative harmony and disharmony in the worlds of form, react upon each other according to the light of intelligence back of them. We say, "As a man thinks, so is he." Similarly, as men think, so are they. As the group thinks, so will it be; as the world of men think, so will be their world. Each thought will produce its reaction, individually upon the individual and en masse upon the mass. In the sensitive atmosphere of the wave patterns responsive to consciousness, no action is ever lost, no thought unrecorded. Each produces its own reaction in accordance with an impartial law without favorites.

As the waves of life-in-form were projected into the labyrinthine shadowland of reflected consciousness, their progress through the maze of oft-misleading forms became dependent upon their growing self-awareness and the unfoldment of their own divine light, an exceedingly slow process once they had become completely immersed in the material murk. They were having to have their attention directed away from themselves, so that in the end they would objectively discover themselves and their true divine nature as an objective reality. They used form to beget form and commenced the seemingly unending struggle to preserve individuality by competing voraciously with other forms. Experience seemed to indicate that preservation of individuality depended upon the repulsion or extinction of other material expressions embodied in form.

Obviously, many cycles of slow development and unfoldment must have been necessary before the relatedness of form became manifest in the interrelatedness of groups, with full harmony between all physical expressions as the final, ideal goal. Having reached the life wave of human form, the ego gradually perceives that any expression of consciousness that hurts another is bound to create a reaction, which is finally destined to prod the individual into an awareness of his error. Two persons in an upper berth may quarrel and disagree as to how they may best sleep, and each may insist selfishly on an arbitrary position. In the end, however, both must realize that the interest of one is the interest of the other and that their solution must be on the basis of mutual harmony, the benign self-interest of wise reflection or the selfless selfishness of perfect understanding—that is, understanding of the "laws" of comfortable sleeping in upper berths!

That which men do to one another, they also do to the expression of the perfect Christ-consciousness behind their shadow-laden understanding and thereby to themselves. So it is the law that every thought and action produces its reaction, according to the extent to which each thought and act is harmonious with the plan of the universe. That plan prohibits—or, more correctly, precludes—hateful, disharmonious expressions of the self without an equal reaction on the self. That is the law of compensation, the law of retribution, of which each soul is its own judge and administrator and the attractor of infinite reminders designed to bring the unfolding form back to the path of wisdom.

It is as impersonal as a machine, but its operation is in no wise mechanistic, for the master of the law works with the law and rules himself according to the law without being mastered by it. The violinist draws a bow over the strings of his instrument and produces sounds that are according to the law of vibrations, the law of action and reaction, the law of compensation, but the harmonies or discords are the personalized expressions of the player. His consciousness is away from, yet governed by, the laws of the mechanism, which itself, in turn, is a creation of—an expression of, an extension of—consciousness according to law. Were it not so, all art would be a problem in mathematics and the building of a symphony the synthetic structure of known formulas. Except, what consciousness would there be to do the knowing? (Of course, some societies have attempted to eliminate the "human element" from their pseudo-scientific scheme entirely and sought to make their art a creature of the machine, but try as they will the effort is still forced and unnatural.)

No one lifetime is great enough to encompass the full meaning of the law, nor is one form sufficient to objectify the true divine harmony of the soul. Hence, it is both natural and desirable that the soul should take on many forms in many ages, gradually perfecting them through experience as objective expressions of the more perfect self.

Advancement through the cycles of reincarnation is always forward, though the necessities of experience may require a return again and again to old environments and situations to guarantee that lessons are well learned; or there may be a momentary glimpse of truth with a later apparent slipping back to apply the lesson in the practical field of experience.

But always there is the promise of ultimate success for everyone; there is salvation for all, while the greatest sin is a failure to learn one's lessons, and the greatest punishment is an opportunity to learn the lessons anew, however painful the process may be.

So says Agasha. How is it accomplished in practical living?

First, by practicing those same simple virtues which have been taught by all great teachers since the beginning of our moral consciousness—friendliness, helpfulness, cooperation, tolerance, honesty in thought and purpose . . . all the attributes of goodness that spell Godliness.

Second, by living as gracefully, graciously and harmoniously, and still as fully, as our life will permit.

Third, by meeting each situation without rebellion,

with patience and, most of all, with understanding—the understanding that seeks to discover meaning and opportunity in every circumstance and every test.

In weighing our experience, we ask ourselves: What does this situation mean to me and to those around me? Is this a test from which I am to derive a lesson and thereby afford myself the chance to grow further toward the Truth; that is, toward a full understanding of the True Way? What may I do, mentally or physically, which will make it a lasting lesson of its kind? Am I weighing this thing in the balance of universal principles or on the limited scales of selfish benefit—a momentary benefit which can be only illusory and ultimately a detriment?

We remember that the record of all of our acts and conduct—even the very act of self-appraisal, the contemplation of our conduct—is kept within our permanent selves, the inextinguishable spark of the Great Self that is our soul. It, like a probing amoeba, seeks expression through many forms, in different climes and through a variety of imperfections of experience to discover the best, the True Way and the perfect form.

By choice, we live in the midst of error and illusion, so that by contrast we may eventually learn of perfect truth and reality; so that we may in the end become aware of the perfection that is our true selves. Therefore, says Agasha, we are not to condemn ourselves or others, but we are to learn from ourselves and others. We are to resist "evil," the negative death-force, not by fearing it or cringing before it, but by becoming that which is its opposite in meaning and spelling, namely, "live"; that is, by being consciously alive—by living positively, learning our lessons and doing good. We are advised to live practically, cheerfully and fully, neither separating ourselves from the world and its practicalities, nor totally immersing ourselves in it without consideration for our advancement in the world of spirit. We do not shun experience, but we learn how we may best alleviate painful experience through realization that pain is a signal of broken laws and lessons unlearned, a stimulus toward positive and harmonious thinking.

Many poets and philosophers have written that it is the manner of our striving, rather than our accomplishing, which counts most. Agasha repeats the admonition. It is the learning we gain from the means, rather than final attainment of a goal in the end that is important—the manner in which we meet our daily lessons and build our awareness of our unfoldment in terms of what he calls the God-consciousness. Graduation, he continually emphasizes, is much less important than the process of self-education which precedes it.

Hence, in schooling ourselves we must all have freedom . . . full freedom of expression in its widest sense (although, naturally, within the practical restrictions of group experience, requiring limited control of those so far below the experience-level of the group that they would unwisely inhibit its advancement). We must have liberty to make mistakes and to profit from our mistakes. In turn, we must have liberty to contemplate our mistakes and perfect self-discipline without duress. It is right to help others, but it is unwise to force unwanted help upon others. It is right to guide, as one might guide a child —avoiding anarchy, yet with a minimum of arbitrary discipline—but it is wrong to attempt to force understanding on others, especially our version of understanding . . . which never can be without some error.

It is impossible for the world of matter to be wholly

without error. So we realize that the greatest good for the greatest number necessarily implies the greatest freedom for the greatest number. The goal of material or so-called economic freedom becomes, in this light, a false goal (the false god, the golden calf), for we are already prisoners of matter. To attain any measure of real material freedom (as Agasha has reminded us in Biblical terms so often), we must first seek spiritual freedom or the "kingdom of heaven," the God-consciousness, which lies within. This is accomplished through our free expressions, personally controlled, and our meditative insight. Then all else shall be added unto us.

To believe otherwise not only is to reverse the cart and the horse; unrealistically it makes the objective of life a valueless, ephemeral, material thing, instead of a lasting, realistic and permanently living experience of the spirit. Again and again we are reminded that it is not reaching the objective that counts most but *how* we reach it—what lessons we have learned along the way, how we have met our tests, what we have learned of the divine purpose and what we have expressed in terms of divine love.

No man can pretend that he has discovered the completely perfect way of living; so he has no right by force to impose his way on society. No man can possess truth. He must be possessed by it, for he cannot possess what is greater than himelf. No one way on this earth can be entirely without error. Were we wise enough to discover it, we would escape the world of shadows and return to the perfect Yolk of Life (again, Agasha's term) from whence we sprung. Therefore, our individual paths toward Truth must all be different, though crossing and recrossing like the variegated warp and weft of a tapestry.

Each of us is weighed in the spiritual consciousness

exactly according to the depth of our awareness and understanding, Agasha teaches. That is true democracy—the democracy of the spirit, which apportions to all the measure of their accomplishment as weighed out by themselves. The right of each to make his own adjustment to the Law of Compensation with as little interference as is practicable from man's laws must remain inviolate in the Plan of the Universe. The instinct toward free expression is born within us, to be an inescapable prod toward understanding. That is why men intuitively feel they must fight tyranny, which is an unnatural interference with the right to err and the right to learn through trial and error. Tyranny, they know, even warps our contemplation of error and so conditions our advancement, holding it to the level of the artificial standards of the tyranny.

Thus, the end does not justify the means. It is the lesson of the means that we must contemplate through freedom of reflection, the all-important free will of self-appraisal and self-realization. The Great Goal urges us on, but the way we attempt to achieve objective perfection, rather than the actual attainment of it, determines our karma. We respect ourselves as individuals and the rights of others as individuals, but as we progress we discover how to mold our individual rights into a pattern of meaning with a minimum of mutual interference.

So Agasha advises us to relax thoroughly and to enjoy life. We learn by living, and if we live wisely we enjoy learning. We help others to learn to live wisely, too, but we do not force such unwelcome help as would harm. We take stock of ourselves each day, recapitulating our errors in an effort to perfect our expressions. We do not castigate ourselves for momentary failures. We simply make note of wherein lies the failure and, pointing our way again toward a truthful goal, try to adjust our life to the Perfect Way, which the Master Teachers of all times and with many symbols have attempted to describe for us. In our kindergarten of life, we learn to face our tests with the knowledge that through them we may gauge our progress and gain the strength to withstand, as well as learn from, any new trials. In this wise do men seek and find, each for himself, their own True Way.

YOU ARE WHAT YOU THINK

IX

Set your affections on things above, not on things on the earth.
For ye are dead; and your life is hid with Christ in God.
—Colossians III: 2-3

THERE ARE MANY inadequate substitutes for right thinking, and practically all of us resort to them at one time or another. Perhaps that is a valid part of our pattern of lessons to be learned through the trial and error of experience; perhaps, again, the resultant penalties are Nature's way of jogging us eventually into a realization that the solution of all problems must come through right thinking.

Certain it is that thought is the incalculable energy-force of the universe, encompassing and pervading all that is tangible to our senses and our comprehension, both in this world and in the worlds beyond. From our reports out of the supra-mundane worlds just above this earth, it is particularly made evident that thought is the control force which must be mastered and which, when properly directed, is capable of molding form, as well as solving all the other problems of a continuing existence.

In that more responsive atmosphere, where the vibrational frequencies have a higher rate than in the denser energy patterns of the earth, the flashing of a thought ray can produce instantly observable results. Confusions and false rationalizations, by one person or by groups of persons, cause reactions which are tangible and visible, whereas the development of a harmonious, ordered mode of contemplating and directing one's life there produces harmony and order in the immediate atmosphere and tends to lift the individual automatically to a less dense, less confused and more orderly plane of life appropriate to his advancement.

These principles, as we should know anyway—though we have to be reminded constantly by teachers wiser than ourselves—are essentially the same, if not so apparent, on the crystalline level we call the earth. Only the degree of the reaction is different. The power to dissipate and mold the heavy crusted thought-stuff is merely less, not totally absent, although we often seem to think it is, judging by our thinking. Of course, our earth learning is excruciatingly slow, and the thought patterns within ourselves and our environment are interminably complicated, conditioned and made over-powering by the accumulations of the past. Still, we have found out some things and are discovering more, which may enable us to appreciate the power of thought.

We are not so aware of thought power as those in the other worlds, because we do not ordinarily see the results in terms of such direct action as persons in the other spheres. We know, however, that invisible radio waves produce patterns of tangible reaction, and we respect their subtle power. Now, too, we are beginning to experiment with brain waves and extra-sensory emanations which are clues to important phenomena going on around us constantly. We are learning that, simply because certain phenomena or their results are not at once observable, we may not dismiss them as inconsequential.

Aside from what we are taught through qualified channels from higher planes, we have established the fact that each material body has an *aura* or atmosphere which is around and extends beyond the physically visible outlines of the body. With appropriate apparatus, we can photograph the human aura, for instance, and there is a musical instrument which may be played merely by waving the hands before it; that is, by introducing changes of "capacity" in the electronic system by mingling the "aura" of the hand with that of the sensitive elements of the instrument. (Radio apparatus has to be shielded from this effect, and television engineers have to cope with the electro-magnetic "shadows" cast by buildings, mountains and other objects.)

Not only do all things, living or inanimate, have such auras, but there are "planes" of vibration or frequency-patterns within the aura for each object, not unlike the multiple layers surrounding the planets. Therefore, say the Agashan teachers, everyone and everything has its ascending scale of vibrational layers, becoming finer and finer and with ever increasing frequency rates as they intermingle with the total environment of the universe. Our living fields have extensions into the higher spiritualized realms, although they are anchored in the grosser atmosphere of the world of forms. The soul itself is an extension of the Yolk of Life, the unfathomable core of existence that some men have called the Absolute, others (like Agasha) the God-consciousness, others the Soul of the Universe. Thus, in the last analysis, everything is boundless and endless, "world without end," all that is.

In the vibrating field that is the aura, those in the spirit realms and clairvoyants here are privileged to observe the luminous effects of changing thought patterns. (The field pattern of an inanimate object tends to remain constant.) The combinations of colors and the layers of tones and coloration likewise are observable with the help of mechanical apparatus, and it is known that states of mental depression, exhilaration, illness, health and all types of mental responses have a profound influence upon the shape and coloring of the human aura. The trained observer can ascertain the mental and physical health, the emotions, the reactions and the spiritual development of an individual by the shades of the various colors and the depth and breadth of the layers in the aura. While it has a basic pattern, variations are constantly being registered in this "light of life," which is the immediate environment of the ego.

The aura, however, is not simply a register for determining the state of mind and physiological well-being of its producer. It is also a depository and a reactor on its own account, as well as an integral zone of the organism. Because it is the most intimately associated of the environments that condition our thinking, it is the most powerful. It has a tremendous reciprocal effect upon all that we express and all that we are, for its light and color not only reflect what we are at a given time but also reflect back upon us so as to produce a cumulative stimulus within our consciousness. Further, the spiritual teachers declare, the aura is not merely the reflection and reflector of our conscious motives and ideals but likewise the clairvoyantly perceptible expression of our subjective or subconscious urges, the hidden accumulations of our false rationalizations, our suppressed yearnings, motives, appetites and fancies. Fixations and frustrations show up clearly in the sensitive vibratory atmosphere of the aura and distinctly magnify all abnormalities in their reaction upon the physical and mental organism.

Where auras are combined into families, groups, communities and nations, it can be understood how powerful becomes the reciprocal force for good or evil. What is worse, the conditioning of the total environment tends to become all too persuasive; that is, we fall easily into the pattern of the prevailing tide, and clear vision through the obscurity of our own darkened atmosphere, combined with the turbulence of the vibratory environment around us, is all but impossible. Only the bright auras of the spiritually illumined or of those striving for illumination by clear thinking stand out like beacons.

Clear, positive, constructive, harmonious thinking, relaxed and devoid of fear—the kind of mental activity that is the most difficult of all of life's processes—tends to cleanse the aura, along with the subjective mentality which so covertly feeds and feeds from the aberrations of the aura. As Agasha has said, "It is a thinking individual who becomes strong and free, and it is a strong individual who can willingly clear his thoughts of the mental burdens placed in his atmosphere by false expressions, false gods and false interpretations. It takes a strong person to stand for that which is wise and to become humble and peaceful within himself. It takes a very strong person to break with tradition and think for himself, so that he may bring forth into his consciousness the wisdom which is already within himself. Only when we break away from tradition and think for ourselves do we begin to grow and release the wisdom of the soul."

The cleansing quality of calm, reflective, meditative

thinking, which seeks meaning in all things, particularly the tests of everyday life, eventually reorganizes the weak, disordered elements of the human atmosphere. By right thinking, we can build a strong magnetic barrier of protective light that will incline us toward all which is good and will provide a tangible bulwark against evil. We may even assist consciously in the formation of such a wall of light around us by visualizing it mentally, says Agasha. Focusing all of our thinking positively (as opposed to what he calls "negative" thinking), we disperse the evilly reacting thought forms which accumulate in our atmosphere. If we do not, these sap our energy, confound our consciousness and compound all of the negative attributes which our thoughts express.

While habit-patterns, both good and bad, or positive and negative, are stored in what Agasha refers to as the subjective part of the brain, their counterparts take definite form in the human atmosphere, both as active entities attaching themselves to the aura and as modifications in the aura itself. Given a certain stimulus, then, these inter-acting forces come into play, and we tend to respond involuntarily according to the patterns, repressions and traditions we have built up since childhood, rather than according to a clear understanding of the problem at hand.

Every man is the sum total of his thoughts, and thoughts are things. They are as substantial as the furniture of our homes, and they wield a power that not only governs our own actions but, in combination with others, creates a kind of charged atmosphere or aura in the environment of a community or group. Hence, we are influenced by the manifold accumulations of many generations besides our own—not simply because of what we have been taught and what we see and hear but by the very real electro-magnetic pattern of the environment itself. This is a fundamental principle not alone of the Agashan philosophy but of the teachings of all great "Masters of Light" who attempt to inspire men to see the "light" by cleansing their thoughts of accumulated darkness. The obscuring blanket of gloom is rendered opaque by the pollutions of wrong thinking. Incredible forces then lurk in the polluted atmosphere.

We are inclined to discount the power of thought whenever it fails directly to move mountains or stones. We regard thought as something which occurs entirely inside of us and has its effects only in our individual actions. Yet modern experimenters have shown (by the "mind-over-matter" experiments with psychokinesis at Duke University and other institutions) that the thought-force does have an external reality. Although it may not always be measurable by electrical meters or gauges, it should be apparent that a powerful relay effect is possible. Such an effect can be compared to the infinitesimally small energy value of a radio impulse. When greatly amplified by power furnished through the receiver, radio waves can produce the full tones of a symphony orchestra, or a picture on a screen, or the responses of a pilotless airplane. We ourselves are both the receivers and transmitters of comparable thought impulses, and these need not be as mighty as a mountain to move it. They need be only of sufficient power to set off the delicate combinations of the relay system within a receptive brain to release the necessary energy for mighty works.

Our task, according to the Agashan teachers, is to place ourselves in tune with the higher, harmonious "white" forces which will release within us finer energies or "light" for wise living, rather than the "black" forces of confusion, disorganization, distortion and destruction. Conditioned as we are by thousands of years of false adjustments to the universal environment, our responses are not easily changed. Most of us are susceptible instruments for the negative, disruptive forces around us. This can be true of whole nations and an entire world, as surely as for a single individual. Our karmic responses, singly and together, in turn add to the time-fettered total burden of mental readjustment. Egos are attracted back to old environments where they have failed before, so they may have another chance to break through the fog of their past misunderstanding into the light; or they are drawn by their souls to areas of new experience to test their readiness for additional understanding. It all operates in a pattern of cycles, a gigantic framework of "wheels within wheels," until the "mills of the gods" grind out our destiny in a way that will best promote conscious awareness of our true selves.

In the meantime, error piles up more error, and the involvements of new karma are added to the failures of the past. Great waves of dark vibration fields contaminate the aura of the earth, and they grow as the thoughts of misguided men continue to feed them. Unless they can be dispersed by the light of positive understanding, their cycles of pain and grief must run their course.

As this is being written, the disturbances in the world atmosphere foretell a new round of violence. The tempo of disintegrating forces is being ever accelerated. Fading hope seems to belie Agasha's promises of a great age of peace (starting around 1965), and the cataclysm of misused thought-power seems ever more palpable. On April 2, 1948, Agasha said: "A black wave [i.e., thought form] hovers over and around Russia; if it continues, they will lose all sense of reason and make it very difficult for all the peoples of the world." This was a characteristic under-statement, but he added: "America will be the leader of all. . . . There will be much to distort and disturb the mentality, but that is our test. Millions will go through these trials, and many will fall victims of the negative thinking of mankind before peace is finally established on earth."

Nevertheless, disharmony in a universal environment of harmony must be a temporary condition. No matter how long the condition may appear to endure in the range of our limited consciousness, the pressure of the universal light will inevitably dispel the gloom of disorder. How soon will depend upon man's purification of his own con-sciousness, according to the laws of cycles, the law of com-pensation, of karma, of action and reaction and the law of evolution through conscious unfoldment.

The significance of mental bodies or thought forms in relation to the whole problem of thought control has been discussed frequently by the Agashan teachers. Closely as-sociated with the aura, these forms to persons viewing them from the spirit side of life are visible representa-tions of our subjective and objective mental activity and in themselves exert a reacting force upon ourselves and our environment. They may be either useful or immeasur-ably detrimental; they may be controlled by us, or they may control us; they may obscure and complicate our way of life, or they may serve to alleviate the problems of our life, all according to the mental force we feed into them or the strength of our resolve to dissipate them.

One of the Agashan teachers explained the phenomena thus:

"A mental body in some cases may be the replica of the physical body, and it can work for you as an invisible helper like any other entity. It reflects and is fed by your thoughts; yet its frequencies react back again on you according to the harmonious or disharmonious nature of your thinking.

"If the objective and the subjective are in harmony, and the individual continues to express harmony in his thinking, this kind of mental body can assist in working out your problems for you. Its vibrations or frequencies, having been established as a thought form by yourself, can react upon you and your whole environment.

"It can either be a force for your protection or a means to your downfall. If it is composed of harmonious vibrations, it will tend to supplement the harmony that is already within yourself. If it is composed of discordant vibrations, the reaction will be detrimental."

A person may create many thought forms, having different shapes and characteristics. Some may look like grotesque representations of the thought force behind them— like distorted people, animals, objects, nightmarish dream figures or outlandish examples of neurotic art. Others may have unusual beauty and coloring, either as abstract thought projections or as idealized forms more conventional in appearance. Should the individual's ruling thoughts be of jealousy, hate, revenge, animosity, malice and avarice, these become fixations which take form and multiply the negative patterns already operative within the individual.

Nor does the cumulative effect end there. Thousands, millions and billions of thought forms are present in the ether, all created by the thinking of individuals and groups who have originated and sent forth these pulsing bundles of energy to do good or evil according to their source. A person is exposed to the suggestive machinations of maliciously directed or vagrant thought forms of low degree when that person's own thought pattern is low or confused. If his thought pattern is harmonious, positive and constructive, the negative forms, whether they be individually created or are the combined expression of a whole group, cannot touch him. He will have his own shield of protective light and will attract good according to his development.

A person's thinking is continually stimulated by the reservoir of past thoughts which have been deposited within the subjective or unconscious mental self. Even when the mind has concluded objectively that positive, harmonious thinking is not only advantageous but necessary, old fears and complexes, grudges and hates, worries and doubts, distrust and animosity may still supply, attract and maintain evil-working entities, which tend to break down the protective shield. Cleansing the inner self and the outer atmosphere may thus become an ages-long process, with attendant travail and suffering. Only a positive, conscious effort to bring about a cleansing through force of will can disperse the noxious mental bodies which abound in a negative environment.

A confused state of mind, especially a fearful or hateful consciousness, Agasha has warned, is an open door to the negative effects of veritable mental monsters which haunt the vibratory atmosphere. Supplied by the aura with the mental "matter" for their formation, the hideous shapes and cloudy distortions of the idea-source present a frightening appearance when viewed clairvoyantly or astrally. The protective answer to the evil they stimulate is a harmonious attitude, not of self-satisfaction, but of visualized happiness, prosperity, joyful health and positive helpfulness.

"Have faith," says Agasha, "that everything good shall come to you and that all that comes to you is for a good purpose—to strengthen your being and to stimulate your understanding through the lessons of experience. Do not give power to that which is evil or negative by recognizing in any way its capacity to harm you. Do not allow the negative thoughts of others to affect you.

"Know that 'I am the way, and I am the light'; that is, the 'I' within you, the real and eternal you. Know that 'I am mighty within myself, for as I think, so am I, and all who come within my range shall feel my radiation and be uplifted.'

"See yourself garbed in a beautiful light, a magnetic field of perfect harmony. Visualize that which is beautiful and helpful, and you yourself shall be helped. There is a law of magnetic attraction which governs the chemistry of these emanations, and you fashion them or cleanse them according to your thought."

One may start the cleansing process by visualizing some happy event or scene of childhood; then this may be followed by all the other pleasant, happy events and scenes which can be recalled. As they are given veritable life and are molded into the pulsating magnetic field of the aura, they become positive ingredients of a mental body having great reciprocal and fortifying power. Replace the shopworn negative thought as it emerges into consciousness, and the positive will eventually be in command, the negative thought forms supplanted and dispersed.

The protective technique can bring about even more substantial results by mentally seeing oneself enclosed in a kind of spiritual sheath of perfect light, preferably white, blue, gold or purple or any harmonious combination of a high vibratory order. The thoughts which create this sheath are not self-righteously expressed but envision perfect health, happiness, harmony and love. When disturbances occur, either in the physical body or in the external environment, the protective armor is more necessary than ever and is reinforced by a relaxed, contemplative effort to realize the meaning of the disturbance—as a test or a lesson, or as the result of some violation of natural law. Thoughts of rebellion and complaint, difficult as they are for all of us to avoid, produce negative reactions that tend to reduce the insulative power of the shield. The finer thought bodies, composed of a glowing essence which radiates a power of its own, are broken up by confused, negative thinking, along with the protective light of the reinforced aura.

Mental bodies need not always remain in contact with the originating individual or group. They may be fed by the originators and sent out to do good or evil, depending upon the susceptibility of the subject likely to be affected. That, in turn, is governed by the texture, pattern, coloring and frequency combination of the mental atmosphere into which the thought form migrates. The aura involved may be the emanating electro-mental field of one person or of two or more whose atmospheres interact and interconnect as the result of similarity and close association. A person having a low grade mental field may in many cases benefit by the higher frequencies he encounters. The helpful reaction, however, usually depends upon the person's readiness to respond or upon his recognition of a change for the better. He can thus be stimulated to augment the higher exterior force of the thought body with internal mental reform. In that case, there cannot fail to be some improvement in his mental or physical condition, despite the fact that he is ever bounded by the cycles of his karma and the unresolved problems of his past errors.

It is through the employment of mental bodies and focused thinking, Agasha has explained, that "absent treatments" are possible. The operator visualizes the ill person as having a perfect and ideally functioning physical body. Or if the person being treated is weighted down with some other difficulty, he is mentally seen working out the problem in an ideally harmonious manner. By this procedure, thought forms are generated and transmitted to mingle with the afflicted one's atmosphere, bringing about results in accordance with the restrictive factors mentioned above. The receiver may not be objectively aware of the helpful broadcasting, but the transmission will be as effective, first, as the positive power of the broadcast radiations themselves and, second, according to the receptivity of the mind for which they are intended. In any event, there must be a natural or willful inclination on the part of the receiver to amplify and build into positive performance what has been either consciously or unconsciously received.

The actual results are sometimes dramatic, as anyone familiar with the history of spiritual healing knows well. Numerous cases of healing have been observed and testified to in the work of Richard Zenor's forces, and there is constant emphasis upon the beneficial results to be obtained by right thinking. Obviously, too, the production of thought forms and aura modifications within one's own atmosphere can in many instances bring about self-healing and self-help, although more particularly where the conscious power is without tension and is not overruled by the lesson demands of accumulated karma.

On the other hand, negative thought forms are drawn to an appropriately tuned receiver like a magnet. The receiver-personality who has attuned himself to gross or negative wave lengths, so to speak, will surely magnify his trouble. The positively attuned, high wave-length receiver will just as surely benefit from the high quality radiations of the universe as a whole and from helpful thought forms in his immediate atmosphere. He is more in resonance with universal harmony and with harmonious mental bodies which are attracted to him. At the same time, he is a transmitter of the same quality of high frequencies. Moreover, a re-tuned receiver-personality, whose "dialing" has been changed to a higher, finer frequency range, will begin to cleanse himself of the complexes and fixations, the troublesome habit-patterns and disorders, which formerly bedeviled him. Even one's dream life, bubbling forth dark messages from the subjective consciousness, can be gradually purified of its pollutions.

In short, we can either choose to create new disharmonies and compound old ones through negative thinking, or we can attract and send forth positive radiations that will be of assistance to ourselves and to others as well, not excluding persons wrapped in a low vibrational field. The positively charged aura will be protected from negative thought forms and auras; the negative aura will enevitably be influenced by the presence of all mental bodies and auras, but especially those of a low frequency.

The words "negative" and "positive" as used in this connection by the teachers should be understood to convey the idea of disruptive, confused vibrational forces, as opposed to ordered, harmonized vibrations. We can make these forces and thought forms our servants, or they can become our masters, because they are directly the products of our mental activity, according to Agasha. It behooves us to realize at all times that idle words, destructive thoughts, injurious acts and hateful impulses are inescapably accompanied by disturbances in the electro-mental atmosphere and will inevitably "react like a boomerang" (the teacher's own phrase), whereas a positive application and materialization of every principle which is beautiful, constructive and good must likewise bring its just reward.

As wisdom is filtered down to us through the various planes of consciousness and finally reaches our level of understanding, we have to interpret and express our ideas of truth in terms of the environment in which we live; that is, we try to understand by depicting principles in terms of the images and symbols with which we are familiar. Consequently, we often perceive the outlines of what is universally true but so restrict our interpretations and applications that the little we do comprehend becomes obscure and distorted.

So it is that, since we ordinarily do not see thought, we are likely sometimes to imagine a mental world to be a void of misty nothingness, completely unrelated to matter and form. At the other extreme, having arrived at the reasonable conclusion that everything is an expression of consciousness and that the individual consciousness is but an undivorced vortex in a sea of mind power, we may decide that matter is a sort of nothingness, an unreality dreamed up by ourselves. The truth, as taught in the Agashan philosophy, more nearly coincides with this last statement, except that we are liable to assume from it that matter is objectively non-existent and without significance.

Any such mistaken idea can only postpone the self-education and enlightenment which our current phase of evolution within the realm of matter is designed to promote, says Agasha.

Matter and form are the expressions of our individual, group and world consciousness within the evolutionary pattern of our present life wave, he explains. They are as real as mind power itself; as real as life, and as significant to our progression as all experience. Although shadows of ourselves and of our level of world-consciousness, matter and form, therefore, are neither to be despised nor ignored, any more than they are to be worshiped and exalted. They are the crystallizations of the great aura of life itself and, centering in the physical body, constitute our vehicle on the path of objective self-awareness. Most important, they are subject to universal laws and are as complexly varied and blended by the operation of the Law within our individual consciousness as thought itself.

Shadows are not beyond the Law, and they are not beyond a profound significance in our comprehension of universal law. Even the most fantastic of our fantasies are subject to law. And their impact makes some impression on our unfolding consciousness, for better or for worse, in something of the same manner as the shadows on a moving picture screen. These shadows, too, are projected according to certain rules and physical laws. Yet, because they are only shadows, we do not disclaim their existence and pronounce them unreal. We do not fail, either, to appraise them in terms of art and beauty simply because such intangible qualities are therein restricted by the laws of mechanics. The soul of the artist transcends the inanimate mechanism of the screen, while remaining inseparable from it. The mechanism becomes a channel of expression, inadequate or superb according to the ingenuity and understanding of the consciousness which directs it.

All through the cycles of our lives we are intimately concerned with shadowy extensions of consciousness. Thoughts take form in many ways, for which we are strictly accountable. Being objective representations of our present state of advancement toward reality, they are only relatively unreal. Mental phenomena do not occur in a vacuum of unconditioned spirituality, either in this world or in the worlds beyond. There continue to be mechanisms and vehicles which are the instruments of strict natural laws until we have finally mastered the lessons of form. They may in the last analysis be more illusion than reality, but we are literally living with our illusions, which in an ages-long journey we must learn to control with our free will.

Pain is the signal of the unlearned lesson, of error due to imbalance in the patterned form of our consciousness. The solution is not denial but understanding, Agasha has stated emphatically. He has also stated that to deny the existence and meaning of the complicated chemistry of physical expression is not only "sinful" (i.e., the error of misunderstanding) but entirely impractical, if we are to grow and learn. Illusive as are the final meanings of our expressions—the shadowy forms which are matter and the mental images in our atmosphere which reflect and broadcast our state of being—they all compose something of the reality we call experience. Matter is the laboratory substance of our learning. It must be as fully accounted for as any other expression of our thinking.

Says Agasha: God intended us to be perfect, and we are perfect in reality—in the reality of our true being. Only our expressions are imperfect. We seem to find it difficult to perfect them and to achieve a perfect reproduction or reflection of our true selves in a given lifetime. So we are forever faced with the lessons necessitated by our trials and errors. If a bodily condition is due to karmic error, we must experience the lesson which the karma has engendered. The measure of our learning will be the extent of our understanding of the principles of life, dependent in turn upon the manner in which we react to the lessons of experience. Theoretically and very often practically, we can avoid harm and certainly we can mitigate and transmute the effects of karma by voluntarily increasing the breadth of our understanding, but our tendency is to find truth and reality through the hard trials of experience.

It is all-important *how* we meet the lessons of experience. If we complain, resent and rebel, we may not only fail to learn the required lesson; we may attract to ourselves new karmic tests of greater intensity. Often our soul-self will require that we repeat the unprofitable experience until we understand its lesson. And denial of the experience is not understanding.

Continues Agasha: God did not intend us to suffer. That is our own intention, the insistence of the soul, which constantly directs, adjusts and attracts experience to bring about a state of individualized awareness of the "God-consciousness." Therefore, it is not contrary to God's law that we should seek to alleviate suffering, correct physical ills and solve individual problems by any practicable means, so long as the end result is a step toward harmonizing our consciousness with the universal God-consciousness. As we harmonize ourselves and transmit harmony to others through the aura and through our mental images, as well as by means of our physical expressions, we can help ourselves and help others to help themselves. We may not pay karma for another, but we may so stimulate harmony in another that his understanding is increased, his lessons are more easily learned and his experience, as a result, is less harsh.

Whenever mental or physical pain signals the message that we have made a mistake or broken a natural law somewhere in the background of our immediate or far-distant past, we are privileged to seek alleviation of the pain by appropriately corrective methods, either mental or physical, or a combination of both. Then we must search within ourselves for an explanation. Perhaps we can identify the mistake and avoid its repetition. Perhaps we shall be able merely to recognize that the error has been recorded in the soul-consciousness and that the soul has attracted to itself a test which will better perfect its expressions. In all cases, we can recognize that there is a lesson to be learned, whether it be one of patience, forbearance, temperance, tolerance or any other moderation of living necessitated by previous excesses. Our goal, as advised by the teachers, should be normal, cheerful, balanced living, a combination of self-restraint without self-condemnation, self-analysis without self-centeredness, internal placidity and tranquility without external apathy and adjustment to environment without fear, hate or complaint, but above all without hate or fear. Fretful worry and fear and hatred of peoples and environment are at the root of many of our physical and mental ills. Transformed, they become love of life and all that is within life. We recognize the world as our great, expanding schoolroom, replete with the privileges, joys and obligations of a wholly equitable and impartial system of self-education.

Nothing can be plainer in the Agashan teachings than that pain is a part of Nature's method—of our soul's method—of schooling us in the art of self-mastery and self-development. Constantly reminding us of error, pain nudges us back onto the true path toward enlightenment. We attempt to correct the error in the most efficient way we know, principally by physical means on the physical level and by mental methods on the mental level. Yet as we advance we learn that right thinking alleviates pain on any level and that certain procedures of thought can work apparent miracles as remarkable as those of Biblical times. Where "miracles" of the mind are not readily accomplished, we may have recourse to physical methods which will relieve the tension and strain so as to pave the way for better, clearer thinking, but if in the end we do not correct the cause, the lesson is intensified and repeated.

We know that in the astral regions, physical ills can be corrected by mental procedures. We are told this demonstrates that the same is possible on the earth level, for we must not forget that the difference between the two states is not of kind but of degree. The same laws apply. It is merely that in the astral the clay of that advanced state of materiality is more plastic, the crystallizations more malleable and responsive to thought power. There the invalid is taught how to take up his bed and walk, if he wills it. As he strengthens his will, the change that he envisions becomes a reality. The vision of health becomes easily fixed in the form which is the astral body.

Usually the readjustment of physical deformities occurs quickly after the astral replica of the body is separated from the earthly form, but in many instances the reality of the defect is so ingrained in the mental processes that it persists in the astral form for some time. Denial of its existence could bring temporary relief, because the force of negation would tend to cancel the outward semblance of the ill. However, the mental image of the defect would remain submerged in the consciousness and might re-emerge in the same or another shape unless a basic principle of thought-power is mastered, namely, that the cleansing of the consciousness is a creative, as well as a dispersive, process of readjustment. That which is elim-inated is put away, not because it did not exist in the ex-perience-world of the objective consciousness, but because its components could be dispersed by the very real force of thought. Creatively, it is replaced by a modification of form—again a reality within the limits of the particular plane of consciousness. The hope is, of course, that the modified form, including its vibrational attributes, will be more congenial to the personality, but such will de-pend upon the ability to operate the mental law.

The same law applies on the earth plane, although the application is not always so obvious nor so visibly spectacu-lar. Men literally build their environments, change the density of their forms and bring into manifestation objects of their concentration in the astral by force of will. In our world, focused thought force can be directed to perform like feats, though in our denser electro-mental atmos-phere and with our lack of training, these "miracles" ap-pear to be more rare.

Nevertheless, we continue to attract to ourselves ex-actly what we are and to transmit from ourselves true re-flections of what we are. We may deny the aberrations of our forms and of our experiences, seemingly removing them from our ken, but the ghosts of their passing linger in our atmosphere until we no longer cling to the errors which gave them birth. Our ills will torment us in one way or another so long as we perpetuate their sources within ourselves. Finally, we learn to shield ourselves within our own kingdom from the disruptive thought force of our environment and at the same time to open the door to the finer thought force which is continually pressing in upon us from the higher planes of consciousness. Wherever the door is opened, this heavenly light, as Agasha calls it, cleanses and purifies like a stream perfecting its channel.

And the key to the opening of the door is absurdly simple: We merely need be conscious of the "heavenly" state, of the fact that there is an infinite power pouring down upon our disturbed atmosphere from realms that consist of ordered concord. We tune ourselves to this light, we are told, by merely being aware of it. That act of thinking in itself is only a beginning, but it is sufficient to raise the level of our consciousness enough to start the process of regeneration and revitalization. From then on, the harmonizing of our consciousness, accompanied by the cleansing of our aura, depends to a great extent upon the consistency with which we maintain our thinking on a high plane. We should have no doubt by this time as to what constitutes negative or destructive thoughts. Our positive, constructive thinking—relaxed, not tense; concentrated but not forced—must flow gently and uniformly to attract to us the vibratory rates of the beautiful and the good. These qualities we seek to visualize in everything we see and do.

We have now taken the first step toward expressing

what the ancient philosophers have called Divine Love. Having taken it, we become suitably responsive to the various messengers of light who are ever ready to help us to overcome our difficulties. We react to their frequencies in a way never before possible. We attract to ourselves more healthful, constructive associations from both worlds. Finally, we eliminate from our personal atmosphere the vampire-like entities which sap our energies and confound our dilemmas. We are, in fact, back on the true road to "salvation."

We do not deny our errors or our faults. Neither do we condemn ourselves for them. We do not deny material experience or shrink from it, for we may not deny its part in our lives without denying its significance as a basic factor in our growth and learning. We do deny its power to harm us in the measure that we express unrestrictive love in our thoughts. We revitalize ourselves and reorganize our living by "raising our vibrations," as the speakers through Richard Zenor put it, by raising the level of our thinking. In this way, we cannot fail to help ourselves, to help others and to be in a position to receive extraordinary help from the higher sources whenever we mentally call for it in an emergency. In that spirit, we may ask, and we surely shall receive—receive the focused rays available to all of us for our help from many sources when we are ready.

Spiritual healing is practical and proven. We can work its wonders ourselves in many ways in the solution of all types of problems. Once having reattuned ourselves, however, we are more likely to be successful in attracting those, either on the earth level or from higher levels, who have developed a thought power which can assist us.

We grow in spirit as we do in body. Once we begin to grow consciously—which means lovingly in the broadest sense—the Way becomes miraculously clearer and smoother. We then may place ourselves in resonance with the vast spiritual resources of the Christ-consciousness.

THE FORCE OF DESTINY

X

Till heaven and earth pass, one jot or one tittle shall in no wise
pass from the law, till all be fulfilled.

—Matthew V: 18

IN THE AGASHAN LECTURES, as we have indicated, physical forms and experiences, are frequently referred
to as "expressions" of the individual or the group. The
choice of this word further implies that our environments
(and the body itself is an environment for the soul) are
reflections of the current stage of our unfoldment.

The body and the intellect, with their accompanying
characteristics and personality, are the immediate "expressions" of the self. One's home is the expression of one's
personality and learning, plus the expressions of other
members of the family and all who have to do with it. A
city is the expression of its inhabitants; a world is the complex expression of the developing group consciousness.
Actions and experiences, likewise, are expressions of the
individual or group, reflecting the depth of their understanding.

These expressions, which are the shadows of our growing consciousness, become ever more refined as we real-

ize objectively what we already know inwardly, namely: that the natural, comfortable, efficiently happy state of the universe is complete harmony. When the expressions of life produce disharmony, reactions upon the ego are inevitable. The all-knowing divine spark we call the soul thereupon attracts to itself such other expressions—environment and experience—as will eventually make the lessons of harmony clear by stimulating understanding. Thus all of our expressions are, over a period of eons, gradually distilled and refined.

When the Adamic man, the great wave of potential consciousness of which we are part, chose to become conscious of wisdom, rather than to be merely in association with it, he figuratively ate from the tree of good and evil and so began his awareness of self through the contrasts of harmony and disharmony. He was "tempted" to do so by the Satanic serpent, the symbol of form, representing the illusion of materiality, which became the shadowland expression of his own evolving consciousness. The serpent is an apt symbol of materiality and of objective wisdom, for all material expressions are combinations of waves and vibrations, and the wriggling snake is a fair representation in animal form of a wave motion. It also represents harmony (an organized system of waves), which is the material essence of externalized wisdom.

Having fallen purposefully from the "Garden of Eden," which is the undelineated state of perfection, the "heavenly home," into the Platonic cave of materiality, the Adamic man could now see the shadowy expressions of himself on the walls of his world-cave and so begin to know himself objectively by interpreting the shadows. Imperfect expressions of himself, he had to learn, were "evil," because they were not truly the reverse of evil—"live." They were not true reflections of his perfect divine nature. He was to discover that his expressions were good, however, to the extent that they reflected the transcendent divine harmony. Certain expressions invariably produced disharmony; others promoted harmony, both within himself and within his external environment. He was to find that the "beautiful and good" are harmonious expressions which produce harmonious reactions; that is evil which, due to misunderstanding, disrupts and disorganizes the normal pattern of true life, the expression of the universal harmony which we recognize as Divine Love.

Because our expressions and our shadowland are an illusion, being only partial and imperfect reflections, we have had to avoid the error of assuming they are not real—real in their capacity as factors of growth and unfoldment, although unreal if regarded as apart from the source. All experience is real, because it becomes a part of our consciousness and vitally affects our development. So, therefore, are the forms with which we surround ourselves real to the extent that they are an integral part of our experience. Experience is the imperfect reality by which we become aware of perfect wisdom. This Agasha reiterates constantly. It is the body of our learning, the tangible aspect of our understanding.

Reincarnation, in turn, is the procedural device which insures continuity of learning and unlimited opportunity for understanding. Its cycles of cause and effect operate inexorably and continually until the individual finally escapes from the wheel of experience by dint of his own understanding. This process generally requires an almost countless number of lives before the realization of the meaning of experience lifts the soul above the maelstrom of material expression. Trying to understand the labyrinthine paths of life, the ego is given the chance to learn the True Way by observing his reflections and the changes that are wrought when he departs from the path.

As his consciousness develops, the trials of learning are commensurate with his understanding, and the penalties for departure from the Way are more formidable. Reactions to wrong action, however, are not so much regarded as punishment but as the granting of an additional opportunity for right action. Yet, the relation of action to reaction does have the quality of the "eye-for-an-eye" code of Hammurabi in its effect, except that it is self-administered. Simply stated, the Law is that no one may do harm to another, nor to himself, without producing a like harm unto himself or an appropriate "review" lesson for himself. Thereby will he learn most directly the effects and meaning of imperfect expression and misunderstanding of the Law.

The thoughts and actions of both individuals and groups produce, in negative form, reactions called *karma*. The person or group producing disharmony will attract a like disharmony in this or a future life and will continue to do so with increasing intensity until the lesson is learned. Thoughts (especially thoughts, for they are a form of action) as well as actions set in motion the law of karma. The wise man produces both within himself through his thoughts and outside himself by his actions the most harmonious expressions of which he is capable.

If the individual has failed to pass all of his tests in one life, he will be attracted back in a new life with an appropriate personality and to an appropriate environment where he may review the unlearned lessons, unhampered by the prejudices and warped interpretations of an objective memory. Yet the soul memory ever remains inextinguishable to guide him.

In the astral world, the individual spends a length of time after a single earth life, absorbing into himself the experiences he has gone through, and then suddenly he "dies" again—the real death, which is a new descent into the realm of crystalline forms on the planet where his life wave is developing. (However, life waves may change planets under certain circumstances, says Agasha.)

He returns as a germ, or a seed, and he animates a new body to which he has been attracted by his soul according to the law of cycles. This decrees—and thus his own soul decrees—that he must go through those experiences which will best stimulate his understanding, and the pattern of his experiences is set by the nature of the environment which attracts him. In practice, he often returns primarily to work out one particular deficiency of character, such as greed or cruelty, but he may create new karma for himself by failing to meet the new set of circumstances with understanding.

The process is long, involved and intricate. The results of each experience are registered in the soul itself and remain a permanent record which inspires the ego to seek new, often horribly painful, experiences for the sake of ultimate realization. For this reason, even the experiences of a child, attracted by past karma, are not lost in their effect, being recorded and absorbed and added to the vast amount of learning which all must acquire to attain universal wisdom.

We earn all we learn by the quality of our expressions, says Agasha, and nothing is added to us but that which we have earned. Always the cycles of destiny continue in this fashion: The soul germ is born to the parents and into the environment best suited to its current phase of development. It takes on personality, the power of observation and sooner or later the power of reflection. After a lifetime in which its powers are used badly or wisely, there is a graduation into the spirit world, where development and unfoldment continue until a new "death" strips it of all spiritual bodies and returns it again to a new temporary home in the earthly Hades.

That mental and physical pain is a vital factor in this process can well be seen, but pain is ever mitigated by the quality of will and its preoccupation with the prime duty of objective understanding, just as when we heed the signals of pain in bodily illness and take steps to correct the physical disharmony which is causing the pain. Finally the lessons of pain, the refinement of personalities and the power of reflection on the meaning of it all— through the exercise of the will—cannot fail to send the soul back to a supernal state beyond the earthly planes . . . not that even then there is any end in sight (there is in reality, says Agasha, no beginning or end), but the quality of perfected existence in the spheres of paradise has the added aspects of self-awareness and compassion. Such compassion requires a deep concern with the progress of all others not so far along on the path who need and are ready to accept the help for which their soul-learning has equipped them.

God helps those who help themselves—but He also helps those who help others. He operates through many helpers, and as we become one of these, aiding those who are willing and ready to be aided, we help ourselves to achieve the end of karma and so attract to ourselves the harmony of perfection.

There is a great temptation among the uninformed to confuse destiny with fatalism and futility. Actually it is the instrument of individual responsibility, not an escape from it. The force of destiny, both according to the ancient teachings and the Agashan, is strictly the creature of the soul and not its master.

First, the soul, in combination with all other points of developing consciousness in its particular light wave, projects itself into the revolving, evolving field of the material universe. Then ensues the complicated process of action and reaction among the pulsing vibrations of the material forms. So long as awareness is negligible—awareness of self and of the relatedness of selves—the reactions to action and consciousness are almost mechanical in their interplay. The entity struggles for unfoldment in contention with the endless combinations of wave patterns that are designed to jar it into a realization of identity and its true self.

By this we mean to indicate that the shadowland of imperfect soul-reflections we call matter is not without its own tendencies toward harmony and regularity, as surely as the rising and setting of the sun, the phases of the moon and the revolutions of the planets. Yet in this arena of form, particularly its lower levels on and directly above the earth plane, the tendency toward the disruption of smaller natural cycles is promoted by a shifting and crowding of consciousness as a part of the vital search for individual expression.

The search involves contentions and collisions among the expressions of consciousness and between these and the so-called natural elements, which are expressions of a world-consciousness slowly evolving in the universal environment. For instance, individuals will hurt and kill one another to win sustenance. Then they will organize into tribes upon realizing that a tribal program is more effective for winning food and shelter, but will war against other tribes which threaten the sources of supply. As realization of the efficiency of cooperation progresses, the cooperating groups become larger, but wherever the individual or the group sets in motion the vibrations of disharmony, either one against the other or group against group, it is as inevitable as the rising and falling of the tides that a reaction must some day engulf each or all to the exact extent that the vibratory atmosphere has been disorganized.

For whatever is done to another is done to the individual himself and to his environment by the creation of a state of vibratory imbalance. Like water that seeks a common level, like the snapping of a rubber band, like the falling of a stone after it is thrown, the force of the universe is brought to bear to correct imbalance. In the material world, the quivering, clashing discordances produced by the misguided struggles of a churning sea of evolving entities must result in an infinitude of combinations of dissonance before each entity finally discovers the peaceful, harmonious relationship which ultimately will and must result.

The restriction on the achievement of this ideal, however, is related to the Agashan statement of the purpose of life, namely, the search for individual awareness of the place of the self in the design of the universe. This means that each individual must come to the realization *by his own efforts.* He must, as Agasha states it, "earn every step of the way." Restrictions may be placed on his actions, great influence may be exerted over his learning, and the extent of his understanding may be profoundly modified and limited by his environment, but in the end he alone can achieve any measure of understanding.

Restrictive systems can never force understanding and, as they inhibit reflection, they inhibit the development of individual expressions which must always be the basis of understanding. The divine realization must be reached freely and voluntarily by reflection upon the mistakes and lessons of experience, which are naturally regimented by the inexorable laws of action and reaction, cause and effect and karma and compensation but unnaturally by the selfish will of men. The imposition of artificial restrictions, then, must be kept at a minimum to provide the widest area of development for the individual, who must have considerable freedom to make the mistakes that are the basic ingredient of learning through experience. By realizing his interdependence with his fellows, however, he voluntarily ranges himself with them, according to his understanding, for the purpose of making certain that the liberty required for his development is truly unhampered within the compass of the Way and the Law.

It is apparent that those systems which least restrict the individual and permit a breadth of expression commensurate with his inclination toward the harmony of Divine Love will encourage the greatest development of peace, harmony and love. Since no material system is perfect, however, the individual within it, as well as the group, is ever susceptible to the pitfalls of willful disharmony— belligerency, hate, revenge, avarice and excesses of all kinds—with the result that Nature exerts her inevitable pressure to correct the imbalance, either within the individual or the group, or both.

The correction of imbalance by means of the law of karma and compensation therefore produces certain foreshadowed results by reason of the individual's lack of understanding. If he understood, like the pair in the upper berth, that harmony is not only desirable but self-ishly necessary, his thoughts and actions would reflect his understanding. He is free, says Agasha, to choose between a course which is along the path toward natural harmony or one which must lead to disharmony. But though the odds may be thousands to one that he will be stimulated by "force of circumstance" to choose the course of discord, he is made uncomfortable enough by repeated mistakes of the same type that he finally learns the lesson of love and harmony.

It is this freedom of choice and, particularly, freedom of reflection which defeats the futile escapism of fatal-istic philosophy. A combination of events may be inevi-table in a given lifetime because of the karma accumu-lated in past lifetimes, but we are ever free to reflect upon the experience and to strengthen our character for the future by refusing to be drawn into the whirlpool of error which may attract new and possibly more painful karma. Nature, it is said, nudges us once to remind us we have mistakenly left the path. Next time, she pushes us if we repeat the mistake. A third time, she shoves us violently, and thereafter the reactions are ever more violent until we have learned wherein we were in error. And Nature, according to Agasha, is really ourselves, our God-self, the divine soul, which is guiding us through the realm of expressions until we have reached a perfect understanding.

Our will is as free as our choice and our power of reflec-tion, and we are assured by the Agashan teachers that there is a wide range of choice, even in a karma-filled life-time. Our greatest exercise of free will, however, they emphasize over and over, is the ability to reflect upon and to learn from all experience, particularly that which is most painful or uncomfortable. Understanding is the perfect balm which will ever alleviate suffering.

"As a man thinks, so is he." This is the ancient axiom, repeated often by the teachers, and in our thinking we finally master the lessons of karma by understanding their significance in our development. The lessons are many and the path a round of many lives, but the Cycle of Necessity, the soul-inspired urge for self-understanding, eventually is fulfilled by a combination of good thoughts and good deeds, which, in turn, must ever be an inspiration to others to reflect upon their own unfoldment and progress toward perfection of expression.

He who helps another helps himself, and he is ready for help who is ready to help another, since both must realize that the rhythms of the universe are antagonistic to disharmony and that the replacement of discord with love must always benefit all. None of us have fully learned our lessons, but our failures are only temporary and our ultimate success spurred on, rather than inhibited, by the Force of Destiny.

EVENTS THAT CAST THEIR
SHADOWS BEFORE

XI

Quench not the Spirit. Despise not prophesying. Prove all things;
hold fast that which is good.

—I Thessalonians V: 19-21

IN THE NATURE of things, as explained by the Agashan
teachers, there is a pattern—or, rather, a complexity
of patterns—of changing events which fulfill the universal
law of cause and effect and the law of cycles. Not all
events, however, are the reactions resulting from long-
due karma. Moreover, events may be shifted and modified by the operation of the will, depending upon the extent to which the will has become the expression of an
awakened consciousness capable of reflecting upon the
meaning of events in the patterns of life.

One can understand that general trends and great social
changes, securely rooted in the karma of the past, would
be difficult to modify. Peoples and nations must fulfill
their karma, as well as individuals, and enlightenment—
the kind of enlightenment that absorbs the shock of inevitable reaction—does not come easily. We achieve but
slowly the kind of enlightenment that enables us even

partially to control the material forces of nature; more slowly do we develop the internal harmony which is the literal manifestation of spiritual light. In the physical world and in the spiritual, light has a regularity of vibration such that any interference with its patterned harmony causes relative darkness.

Coming events, therefore, must always cast their shadows before, for they represent a modification of the basic vibrational harmony of the universe. On the earth plane, the modifications often become a confusion of pulsing, whirling interdependent eddies in the sea of etheric force (again used as an arbitrary, illustrative term) that has been molded by unfolding spirit in the worlds of form.

Most of our lives are spent trying to interpret the advance warnings of new events. We budget our economy by predicting our expenditures; we plan our laws on the basis of predictions as to their need and effect; we construct great projects on the basis of probable utility; we forecast the weather scientifically, and we develop a mathematical science of probabilities to help us plan for the future in many areas of endeavor.

These are "recognized" methods of prediction. Among persons with psychic gifts, a comparative few have the ability to interpet the wave motions of cause and effect around them and to translate them into pictures of coming events with fair accuracy. Some persons in the spirit world also have this gift, but *not all*. Mere existence in the after-death world no more bestows the gift of prophecy than the spirit of wisdom. I have several score recordings of prophecies by various discarnate personalities, speaking through the inter-world telephone provided by Richard Zenor. The statements vary from examples of astonishing accuracy to clear misses or practical unintelligibility.

There are enough "hits," however, to demonstrate beyond doubt that it is possible to predict specific events. Yet the best prophets almost always mention the uncertainty of any particular prediction, due to constant changes in cause-and-effect patterns, especially in the case of relatively minor events on the individual level. Besides, hosts of "guides," "messengers," "angels of light" and organized brotherhoods in the spirit worlds are continually working , we are told, to alleviate the confusions of earthly life by projecting into it harmonious rays of spiritualized light and also by inspiring those whose development is capable of being stimulated through the higher thought-force. Karmic responsibilities and conditions tend to set the pattern of major events for both the individual and the group, says Agasha, but the crystallization of pattern is never completely static. Therefore, the prophet, like some branches of science, deals with probability factors, as distinguished from fatal necessity.

For instance, on August 24, 1945, a person calling herself Genevieve Clearwater spoke the following words through Mr. Zenor in the course of giving a number of prophecies:

"I hear an explosion, and it seems to be not too far from the city of Los Angeles. It looks as though it is along the water front, or it looks as though it comes from some oil district, but as I sense it and as I have seen it in my meditations over here, *it doesn't seem to be avoidable.* However, there may be a few killed and much damage, but it appears it has something to do with oil or oil wells. Anyhow, it appears that what they're working on, such as gasoline and of the like—new gasoline and of the like— it appears that they must be extremely careful, because there is an explosion. *However, we hope it can be avoided, but we just don't know. It is seen here in the vibration."*

Six days later, on August 30, 1945, a page one headline in the Los Angeles *Times* read:

"Oil Well Blast Kills Six at Seal Beach; Force of Explosion Jars Whole Area; No Witnesses Left."

The story began:

"Five men were killed instantly and a sixth died soon after in a giant flash explosion which wrecked an oil derrick of Shell Oil Co., Inc., east of Seal Beach yesterday and sent a sheet of flame 1000 feet into the sky."

The article explained that the men were preparing for a "production test" on the new well, which was near the ocean front in the Seal Beach district, not far from Los Angeles.

Often those attempting a prophecy are able to pick out happenings that would seem to require an astounding combination of chance circumstances to fulfill. Often, too, they struggle for words to describe the scene which their clairvoyant vision has created for them, and much of the art of prophecy lies in a rare gift of descriptive words. Few have it, and many who attempt a demonstration are vague or unintentionally incoherent in trying to make sense from what at the moment has no apparent meaning.

Following is a quite skillfully worded description given through Mr. Zenor and disc-recorded by me on August 3, 1945, around the time that the name of Major Richard I. Bong, Pacific war ace, was much in the news:

"One very important person as far as aeronautics is concerned, it appears to me, is losing his life because he apparently has great ambition to fly one of the new planes, and somehow or other he doesn't fly it properly, or something goes wrong, and he loses his life. It is not too far distant."

Major Bong, holder of the Congressional Medal and credited with downing 40 Japanese planes in the South Pacific, was killed only three days later on August 6, 1945, when he flew a new type P-80 jet-propelled craft over the San Fernando Valley in the Los Angeles area. The ship, it was reported, exploded in the air. It then crashed in a vacant lot.

Two months previously Major Bong had told a journalistic fraternity meeting of his great desire to fly the new plane and his "high hopes" for it.

This prediction, incidentally, almost caused trouble for one young lady. She heard the prophecy on the night of August 3 and immediately connected it with Bong. She was an employee of Lockheed Aircraft Corporation, from whose field Bong took off. It was apparent that he was in difficulties when the ship passed the control tower of the field; so when someone in the office where she worked received a call from the tower that Bong was "about to crash," she exclaimed almost involuntarily that she had known it for three days.

She succeeded finally in convincing company investigators and the F.B.I. that she was not an enemy agent but was merely "psychic."

Impending tragedy seems to mark the psychic atmosphere most vividly, but frequently events that are little more than trivial and have the appearance of complete fortuity are forecast. On January 5, 1945, I made a recording of this prophecy a fortnight before it came true:

"There seems as though I see here an automobile moving along, and it seems like this automobile is trying to deceive the airplane, and the airplane is trying to dodge it, and it's trying to run faster, but they seem to crash at an intersection. That seems to come here in the southern part of California not very far off."

Los Angeles newspapers reported the event on January 20, 1945. A P-38, having overshot the runway at an army airfield in the San Fernando Valley, almost wrecked an automobile which was traveling nearby. Luckily the car, which was struck at a valley street intersection, was only slightly damaged, and no one was hurt. The plane plunged through a fence and came to rest off the road.

Time appears to be a very abstruse factor in making predictions, and inaccuracies are often noted. I have among my records two "prophecies," each of which in different words clearly points to the death by suicide of the film star, Lupe Velez. Yet one of these was given before her death, and the other, afterward. In each case, the speaker seems to be trying sincerely to give a clear description of a vibratory picture or impression, but in the case of the second "prediction" the speaker appears completely unaware that the event is passed.

The prophecy made in advance of the event was recorded on September 20, 1944:

"One very mysterious death of a famous movie star is to take place in a short time, mysteriously disappearing out of the body. That will be a flareup here in the next, oh, very short time. I believe it's around the Christmas period. This happens to be a woman, glamorous, very glamorous."

The famous "glamor girl" took her life on December 14, 1944, and the newspaper "flareup," of course, continued for some time, with constant references to the "mystery" of the affair, in spite of a note of explanation left by the actress.

The second "prophecy" contained similar language, with the added information that the famous person would take her own life because of some personal involvement. Yet the prophecy had already been fulfilled.

Philosophically, as has been argued by wiser heads than mine, an event has neither a beginning nor an end. It has transitions, transformations, mutations, variations, precessions and successions, but all are interwoven and intermingled without a definitive start or finish. Looking backward along the path of a related sequence, of course, is much easier than looking forward along the line of probabilities and related variables. Yet even ordinary men can sometimes see or sense the trend of events (strictly, no doubt, we should say, in the singular, "trend of event") that forecast vital and general transformations.

In this day, many types of prognosticators have sprung up to diffuse a little light or, on the other hand, to confound confusion by plaguing the unwary. These prophets and pseudo-prophets range from editors of business letters to radio commentators, many of whom make a practice of selling tiny peeks through the veil of the future according to their lights. The only difference between their kind and the psychic kind of prognosticator is that the latter claims to have "inside information" not immediately available to the more materially minded. The psychics contend that they are more sensitive to the subtle wave motions of concatenating events. Therefore, they are better equipped to predict specific results from basic causes, depending upon their ability to express themselves and to interpret the pictures these wave patterns stimulate in their psychic vision.

As the prophetess called Genevieve once put it:

"In making predictions—many of which have material-
ized, as you know—we are able to pick up these vibrations
because we can see on the inner planes, the psychic planes
or the mental planes. We know what people are creating
which will cause the result which we see. We see the result of causes they set in motion, that is all, and that is
how we are apparently able to 'see' things in advance."

Since each person and, in fact, each atom has its extensions into the etheric planes, all change is recorded there.
By tuning in the frequency of the recording planes, the
psychic often can view the literal shape of things to come
as projected from the patterned causes of the past.

It is becoming widely recognized that all of us have
some psychic ability, although for the majority it is
largely submerged. Experiments with dreams, for example, have demonstrated that careful notations of all
that is remembered immediately upon awakening will
include a hodge-podge of symbols and pictured facts,
with some of these discovered to be clearly related to past
and others to future happenings. The experiments in
clairvoyance or extra-sensory perception also have brought
to light latent abilities to "predict" with some accuracy
the card order in an ESP arrangement. Extensive "precognition" tests have been conducted with positive results by Dr. J. B. Rhine at Duke University (cf., his
The Reach of the Mind, William Sloane Associates, Inc.,
New York, 1948) and by researchers elsewhere.

Other experiments with telepathy have produced astounding examples of prophecy, when no such results were
sought or anticipated—notations by the receiver who
thought he was getting direct communication, rather than
shadow images of the future.

In my own experience, I have found an unexpected ability to receive occasional and sporadic impressions of future events, notably while completely relaxed and just before going to sleep or upon awakening. I made the discovery while attempting the type of dream-recording experiment mentioned above. As is true of so many other "prophets," I soon realized that I could never predict what I was going to predict or *if* I was going to predict; that is, there seems to be little control over the nature of the prediction—at least, none in my case. Seemingly irrelevant flashes or mental pictures come without warning and without a clear indication of their ultimate significance. Whether they were sense or nonsense was not immediately apparent.

During the time I was actively interested in this type of experiment, I found that the mental flashes sometimes were in the form of words or phrases, as well as pictures. Names were not infrequent—names of persons whom I later met but had no idea they existed at the time the impression was noted.

The specific detail of the picture-visions was especially interesting. Two typical notations:

"Native girl with water jar on head, smiling broadly and doing kind of military salute."

"Native handing me a rose."

I have photos of both of these scenes, taken in Cairo more than a year after the "visions" occurred. The native girl was one of two I photographed together at a public well. My dragoman asked them to pose, and just as I took the picture, one—still with her water jar on her head—snapped to mock attention, smiled very broadly indeed and raised her hand to her head in a palm-out salute. The gesture was entirely without prompting of any kind and without warning, although suggested no doubt by the presence of large numbers of British troops in Egypt at that time (late 1939, after the outbreak of the war in Europe).

The rose incident also occurred in Cairo when a galabia-clad gardener suddenly cut and handed me the flower while I was being shown about the grounds of the Egyptian University. Since my camera was already in position, I caught the incident on my film.

A few days later, while discussing mental phenomena with an archaeologist friend, I mentioned that I had experienced several instances of apparent precognition during my trip. I said that in one vision-flash I had pictured myself standing beside what seemed to be a large hedge of "California-type cactus" (as I put it). The prickly plant seemed to be associated with Egypt, rather than California, and I drew for him a rough sketch of the form of the cactus—large round or oval "leaves" joined as in a chain and covered with sharp spines.

My friend said he did not know of any plant of this type in Egypt, although he showed me a few varieties he was growing in small earthen pots. About a week afterward, however, I found the hedge alongside a canal in the Nile Delta, after some other friends and I stopped for a picnic lunch. It was just as I had "seen" it in advance, very California-like and higher than the tallest in the party. I was able to send a photo of it to the archaeologist.

Since numerous predictions through Richard Zenor parallel later printed headlines or accounts, I will mention two other personal experiences to show that this universal but generally latent power of second-sight can extend both to events and the recorded references to events.

Considerably more than a year prior to Franklin D.

Roosevelt's death, I received a mental picture of a headline in a particular newspaper, the Los Angeles *Examiner*. I was able to see the *Examiner* masthead and the glaring black words: ROOSEVELT DIES.

On the afternoon the news was received in Los Angeles, I mentioned this "dream" to two friends, Miss Nadine Mason of the Los Angeles *Times* and Mr. Bernard Weissman of the *Examiner* (I was with the Los Angeles *Evening Herald and Express*). I remarked, since we were all away from our offices, that it would be interesting to see what the headline in the *Examiner*, a morning paper, would be.

This conversation occurred while we were all en route home but ahead of the publication time for the first morning editions. The following day we jointly confirmed that the early editions of the *Examiner* were the only newspapers in the Los Angeles area, at least in the metropolitan field, which carried as their main headline the particular wording: ROOSEVELT DIES. All other newspapers, so far as we could determine, including the evening papers, used other phraseology.

Following is the other example of an apparent mirroring in advance of a "reproduced event":

On the night of November 24, 1944, I received such a vivid impression of a peculiar scene that I wrote down a quick description.

"Man (or person) stands on one end of a teeter-board and jumps on it in such a way that some sort of figure on the other end is bounced through the air and he catches this figure."

I even made a crude line drawing to illustrate the idea.

Five days later I walked into my office to find my photographer, Mr. Albert Smith, and several others clustered around a magazine, admiring the craftsmanship of a series of action pictures. I was flabbergasted to discover that the layout depicted my quasi-dream scene completely, except that there were more figures and a slightly more complicated form of action than I had described. However, the teeter-board was there; the acrobatic performers were there, and their stunt was to bounce one of the acrobats onto the shoulders of another—so as to land atop a sort of human totem pole, instead of being returned to the original jumper, as I had indicated.

A careful check was made of the distribution facilities of this magazine, and it was found that it was not placed on sale in Los Angeles until four days after my notation, or one day prior to the incident in the office.

I am convinced that I "saw" the scene correctly in advance; my failure of complete accuracy, like that of many another "prophet," was one of expression—imperfection of wording my impressions—rather than of vision. I do not mean to say that clairvoyant visions are always accurate or always clear, but many times the difficulty of confirmation lies in the fact that the description of the vision has been poorly or inadequately phrased.

Mr. Zenor has demonstrated considerable clairvoyant ability on his own account, apart from his trance mediumship. The following especially quaint story was told to me in 1937 by a young woman who had known him since childhood:

"A number of years ago when Richard was still a little boy, he made some predictions for me. He said he saw me in a green dress and said that I would receive a parrot—a little green parrot. He said he saw me holding the parrot and laughing.

"He also said I would get a Persian cat and a little brown dog.

"Within six months, all of these predictions came true. I had a yellow dress which I dyed—or tried to dye—blue. Instead, it turned out a bright green. The first time I put on this dress—while I was putting it on—a little green parakeet flew up to the screen of my window outside. I opened the screen and let it in, and it perched on my finger.

"I went with it into another room to show my mother. It was still perched on my finger, and I was laughing so hard I couldn't talk. Mother saw me and exclaimed, 'Why, that's just what Richard predicted!'

"A little later we were at the home of friends, and there was a beautiful Persian cat walking about. They said they didn't know whose cat it was but that it had been staying there for several days. They asked me if I wanted it. So I took it.

"I was in San Francisco some time after that, and a friend gave me a little brown dog—a cross between a Pomeranian and a fox terrier."

In the spirit worlds, the individual is divested of some of the material corrosions which tend to dim the "second sight" of most of us who are still in the physical shell. Depending upon development, native ability and facility of expression, the spirit prophets can usually make a better showing than the earth-bound forecaster. Moreover, the spirit psychic has access to a wider range of objective information with which to add authentic color to his conclusions. Thus, during the war, those in Richard Zenor's classes were kept well informed, comparatively, as to the progress of the world-wide operations and at the same time were permitted on occasion to glimpse the general nature of likely happenings in the future.

For instance, long before the United States had entered the war, speakers through Mr. Zenor warned of coming Japanese activity along the Pacific Coast, but said that this would be "quickly controlled." Despite some ship sinkings and the firing of a few shells onto beaches, we now know that such activity was, in truth, relatively slight. Similarly, in the European theater, a fairly good advance picture of the situation as it progressed was given by a number of speakers.

For example, on March 9, 1945, a speaker commenting on the German situation said:

"Some awful things are going to come out in the paper as to what they have done, needless to say, but in the next seven days a great turn in the war shall take place."

Almost at that moment, the Americans were beginning to stream across the Rhine at Remagen, after the Germans failed to blow up the Ludendorff bridge. On March 10, the Germans lost an air battle to destroy the bridge; and exactly a week after the prediction, on March 16, news-papers reported the big push across Germany had begun. Third Army tanks, said the dispatches, "broke loose along the Rhine Valley on a 12-mile rampage that was forging a ring of steel around two German armies in the Saar and Palatinate. . . ." This was the start of Patton's devastat-ing armored drive across the Reich. March 16 dispatches also carried a State Department report of "peace feelers" by the enemy through the British legation in Stockholm. It was the great turn in the war.

The "awful things" did not begin to be revealed until the following month when the abominations of Dachau, Belsen and the other Nazi horror camps were discovered by the advancing armies. The reports and headlines, beginning April 15, read like this:

"Ten thousand German political prisoners, about one-half dead and the rest dying, were found at Nordhausen, Germany."

"Yanks Force Nazis to Dig Up Massacre Victims"—April 21.

"Yanks Capture Dachau, Find Trainload of Dead"—April 30.

"Cannibalism Forced on Nazi Camp Inmates"—May 10.

Numbers of "controls" speaking through Mr. Zenor had repeatedly told of the coming development of atomic power, primarily for constructive purposes, long before Hiroshima, but as early as September 15, 1944, they began to speak guardedly of a tremendous secret weapon with such incalculable destructive powers that its use would bring a sudden end of the war.

On September 22, 1944, one prophet referred to "some overnight power that will destroy Japan." On September 29, while discussing German secret weapons, a speaker said, "America has something worse" and referred to it as a "big bomb." By March 3, 1945, we were being told that America could "almost destroy Japan overnight" and, on March 16, that America was ready "in the twinkling of an eye" to turn on a power much worse than any the Germans could devise.

After the German surrender, we were told (on May 25, 1945) that we would be "amazed at how quickly the war will be controlled" and on July 27, the prediction was that there would soon be a "sudden end, almost overnight." A few days later, the bomb was dropped.

Meanwhile, in the early months of 1945, the Zenor prophets over and over promised "startling news" before long about such figures as Hitler, Mussolini, Goering and Goebbels. Here are a few of the remarks and the dates on which they were recorded:

January 12, 1945—"Some very startling news comes out, very important news, about Hitler that the American people have been waiting for."

January 19, 1945—"Relative to Goering, there is an attempt on his life. . . ."

January 26, 1945—"There is some startling news coming out in the paper relative to Hitler, and you will hear of it shortly. I see black letters, and (it is) most startling to the United Nations."

February 23, 1945—"There will be some startling news soon about Goering. Goering is going to do something that is going to completely upset the whole plan, regardless of his superiority in carrying on his war plans. . . . There's some very startling news coming up here soon relative to Hitler that will please America but certainly will displease the German people."

March 16, 1945—"You are going to read some very startling news about Hitler. I can see that in big black letters on the front page, of course, and it seems as though it's startling news and good news, of course, so far as the American people are concerned."

March 23, 1945—"Some startling news will be brought to bear about Hitler, some awful things."

April 20, 1945—"You are going to receive some very important, startling news, as I said before, as far as Hitler is concerned. And also I hear the name and also see the name Goebbels, and you are going to hear some very startling news about him . . . in the very near future."

News of Goering's resignation as head of the German Air Force came on April 26, followed by news of his break with Hitler and the Fuehrer's attempt to execute him. The announcement of Hitler's strange death came on May 1, and subsequently the story of Goebbels' suicide was also told. The full story of the bizarre goings-on between Hitler and Eva Braun, however, had not yet been told by May 11, when strange headlines were promised about "some very peculiar happenings" relative to Hitler.

This pseudo-romantic phase of the dictator's end was obviously the subject of another earlier prediction, which on November 3, 1944, promised:

"Some startling news is to arise soon relative to Hitler, which will be in your papers, and it is quite amazing and likewise amusing to the American people." There followed an error in timing, however, since we were told that the matter "is supposed to come up this month."

Allied victory on all fronts was predicted from the first, and the general timing was indicated with some accuracy. Typical was a statement on March 23, 1945, that "in the next 30 days there is going to be a terrific fall in Europe," with the final end "between now and July."

Good timing also is evident in this one of April 20, 1945:

"The military heads (of Germany) at this time have more or less disbanded. In fact we have reports that some of them have already committed suicide. There are more to take their lives in the next few hours and the next few days."

And a week later, on April 27, 1945, three days before the announcement of Hitler's death:

"Thousands upon thousands have committed suicide. You don't get the news here. You hear very little. In fact some of the important heads—that haven't come out in the paper, that they don't know anything about—have already committed suicide—will come out later. You are going to receive some startling news in a short period about Goering."

It is significant that the reference to Goering was connected with the reports of prominent suicides, although the more immediate "startling news" came with his capture by the Americans on May 8. It was then that the fat Reichsmarshal revealed that he had been under arrest on Hitler's orders at Berchtesgarden and was awaiting execution because he wanted to conclude a surrender to the Allies. He was rescued by members of his Air Force, only to die later by his own hand just before he was to have been hanged with the other top Nazi war criminals.

One more interesting prophecy on the last phases of the German war, this one recorded on April 20, 1945:

"The important military heads are disbanding in Germany now. They are falling and trying to run away. They are trying to disguise themselves, and some of the military heads—you will read about this very soon, two in particular—have disguised themselves so completely that —well, as far as being recognized, it's almost an impossibility, but they will be recognized and through some characteristic or something here. It will be quite startling to the American people—not only startling but quite amusing."

Consider how completely this prophecy was fulfilled, even to the "amusing" details:

May 23, 1945—Julius Streicher, the notorious Jew-baiter, is captured on a farm in Bavaria while disguised as an artist, pretending to daub paint on a landscape scene.

May 24, 1945—"Disguised Hangman Takes Hidden

Poison" (headline in the Los Angeles *Evening Herald and Express,* advertising the capture and suicide of Gestapo Chief Heinrich Himmler).

June 14, 1945—Foreign Minister Joachim von Ribbentrop is captured minus his clothes in a Hamburg boarding house after he had made his way to that city in a disguise.

June 23, 1945—Dr. Eugen Fleiderer, described as "one of the top officials of the Nazi labor front," is found and captured near Leipzig, crouching in a pig pen and carrying two satchels full of labor front pay roll money.

At times the prophet-speakers seem under some compulsion to reveal so much and no more. As a matter of fact, they have stated that, in certain situations, they must conceal as well as reveal, for fear of causing undue alarm or complicating an already difficult situation. For months there had been hints in the predictions that President Roosevelt's health was failing when on March 30, 1945, this was recorded:

"A very important person is going to be freed from the physical body in the White House again, and it appears to come up here fairly soon—a *very* important person, but this person seems to go out of the body very suddenly."

The "again" left room for doubt that the death might be among the White House staff, rather than the president himself, but the word "very" was given special emphasis.

On April 6 the approaching event was thinly disguised in this way:

"You will hear a message come out about President Roosevelt, which is to come out very soon, and it appears that it is going to be rather disturbing as far as Roosevelt is concerned."

His sudden passing came only a few days later, of course.

It is interesting that the record—of a feminine speaker—plainly reproduces a deep sigh and long hesitation after the words "it appears."

Many references naturally were made to Europe's dictators in the predictions. One which linked Mussolini to Hitler was recorded on April 13, 1945:

"Some very important news, undoubtedly startling, will reach the American people in a very short period relative to Hitler. Very strange information shall come out of Germany and through neutral countries, and it appears it is going to be about Hitler and some very disgusting conditions about Mussolini."

Previously another disguised hint of Mussolini's disgusting fate was given on March 9:

"There is some other important news that is going to come to the public's notice about Mussolini, and it is going to be—well, we won't say it's sad, of course not—but it's startling news, or at least it's important. . . ."

Mussolini and his mistress were shot on April 28, 1945. His body later was hung head down from the rafters of a gasoline station in Milan. Still later, the body was kicked and spat upon, and a United Press dispatch of May 1 used the very word which made the April 13 prediction distinctive:

"In contrast to the *disgusting* sight that was Mussolini's face, the girl who sought movie fame remained beautiful in death and disgrace. . . ." Hitler's macabre alliance with his mistress-bride came to light after the announcement of his death on May 2.

As to the whole war picture, this was a recording of March 23, 1945:

"I still maintain one thing—that when the fall of Germany comes that the Japanese campaign is not going to be prolonged, as many people say—going on for several years. Remember that Tokyo can be smashed in a few days—now believe it. It may sound silly, making that statement, but if they want to, they could—can just almost destroy all of Japan overnight, and we know it."

The world knew it when The Bomb was dropped in August.

DARK DAYS AND THE
BRIGHT FUTURE

XII

WE ARE SO OFTEN trapped in the darkness of our confusions and delusions we fail to remember the
ancient truism that it is always darkest just before the
dawn. The Agashan teachers have for many years been
promising both a period of Stygian darkness and an inevitable golden dawn. The Dark Days, the time of the Black
Wave of evil, they said, would be the most trying period
in the history of the earth for thousands of years, but sur-
vivors would find themselves facing an era of ineffable
splendor and advancement.

While most of the recorded predictions in my collection
were short-term forecasts of the more or less immediate
future and were made by psychic specialists from the other
world, the teachers from time to time have given indications in more general terms of what we might expect in
the future on a long-range basis. I can recall as far back
as 1935, when we were in the midst of a depression we
thought was about the worst calamity that could befall
civilization, we were dismayed by the predictions of an
appalling "Black Wave" of war, turbulence and disaster

which they said was still to come. The year 1940 was to mark the beginning of these Dark Days and the Apocalyptic horsemen were to have full sway for the better part of twenty-five years or, with varying degrees of catastrophic revolution, until about 1965.

Late in 1939 I was planning a trip to Europe and, deluded like many by the foibles of the age of appeasement, believed that all the sword rattling was only part of a huge game of political bluff. Man had learned to fear war, and while the dictators were trading on that fear, many of us thought they never really intended to fight. So I went ahead with my plans in the face of repeated predictions through Richard Zenor that war was really coming. (I had not then the advantage of studying so many accurate prophecies.) Finally I tried to get some assurance that there would be no war until after my trip. No, they said; there would be war. It would come soon and last long—ten, possibly twenty years or more. But if I continued with my plans, I could go safely, and I would be protected. The war broke out while I was en route across country to New York. Nevertheless, I managed to continue overseas anyway, and I can recite many small incidents which prove how well I was protected.

As the war progressed and the post-war conflicts took over, those of us who had heard the early prophecies of doom-like calamities realized how well named was the Age of Darkness. Continuous "wars and rumors of wars," multiplying confusions and calamities of mounting proportions, we were warned, were still ahead. We were told, in effect, that we hadn't seen anything yet.

For centuries, prophets of one kind or another had predicted the end of the world. Now at last we began to see that the end of the world was at hand—the end of the world as we had known it. The signs of the end of the old world became ever more apparent. Yet, while scientists and politicians showered us with a frenzy of warnings that man might completely obliterate his material world, the Master Teachers in the indestructible spiritual worlds assured us that catastrophe and adversity were but the pre-dawn prelude to an incredible Golden Age of material and spiritual attainment.

The world, they said, would be so different that it could be regarded as a New World, united in enlightenment and bound closely by material progress. It would, they said, literally be a "Heaven on Earth" in comparison to the turbulent agonies of the times before the rebirth.

The climactic years within the greater range of the modern Dark Age were designated as between 1952 and 1955. By then the ranks of the ignorant oldsters, intent upon preserving the old order of strife, would begin to thin out and younger, wiser leaders would appear on the horizon of hope. The conflicts and confusions would continue with abating intensity until the 1965 dawn, but there would be in the decade from 1950 to 1960 faint rays of the full golden light ahead.

The rule of the Four Horsemen, the rule of conflict and disaster, the rule of evil and darkness during the climactic period of the Black Wave would be a time of testing and a time of cleansing, we were told—a time when perhaps half the world's population would be eliminated by the Juggernaut of accumulating wars and disasters. Not only were men's troubles to be of their own immediate making, the product of their ignorant stupidities and selfish antagonisms, but they were to reach a crescendo as part of a greater karmic cycle that would bring the titanic forces of the sphere itself into play.

Not only would man be plagued by the woes of war and civil strife, starvation, disease and slavery, resulting from his own self-deception and conceit, but the stirring Titans would disturb the very bowels of the planet with mighty spasms of violence. The so-called natural disasters—earthquakes, fires, floods and storms—would add their full measure of fury to the general woe. Over the face of the earth the convulsive forces of change and of preparation were to be let loose as a part of what was termed the "process of elimination." Men with the heart of Job were being prepared for the Golden Dawn.

All life, all action, says Agasha, has purpose. Nothing is without purpose or without significance. So it was told that the trying years of the Great Test were to be integrated into a karmic design that would bring home to man the oft-repeated lessons of past centuries. This was the time for man to prove his learning. This was to be the time of the great examination, the opportunity to contemplate with humility the meaning of compassion and cooperation. The solution to his predicament would be the measure of himself and his readiness for a reign of peace and plenty.

Man was to be given a chance to sublimate his encrusted selfishness and predilection for conflict in the common struggle for existence in the face of common adversity. The time had come when man would be forced, by the extent of his own destructive impulses and the overwhelming weight of universal adversity, to release the tensions which had thrown him out of balance with Nature. To the extent that he submerged both his hates and his fears and cooperated voluntarily in solutions that would accord with natural law, to that extent would his suffering be alleviated, Agasha taught.

Finally, the great test passed and the lessons learned, not by only a few in sparsely lighted corners of the earth but by a mighty many in every land, then would the great Phoenix of the World shake off the ashes of the holocaust and emerge with such a new glory as to reflect the heavens themselves. Man would find in the end that he had sacrificed himself on the altar of selflessness in order to find and save himself. The long promised Light of the World would then become a reality.

These were the predictions of Agasha and the other "Teachers of Light," rather than of the various experts from the higher astral planes—they who tend to specialize in other than long-range prophecies. While these long-term predictions of a Golden Age necessarily were couched in language more general than that used by forecasters of specific events, the same law of cause and effect applies, but it operates on a grand scale and in broad, inclusive sweeps of tide-like reaction that govern all the world and its peoples.

According to the Agashan teachings, man by his actions and, above all, by his thinking, creates the confusions which darken and pollute the earth's psychic atmosphere, thus bringing about a strictly artificial and unnatural condition of oppressive turbidity. The world, too, has its grand karma, and as in the case of all its parts, the law of the cycles must be fulfilled.

Men have spoken and written of the Golden Age, a millennial advent of unsurpassed well-being, of prosperity and spiritual light, since the beginning of history. The hope of a perfected society is reborn in generation after generation and persists as an instinctive drive toward the attainment of a bright but distant goal. That brightness, the promise of a flooding, cleansing, harmonizing light of pervasive brilliance, is no mere literary allusion, says Agasha, but a tangible representation of the one, the beautiful and the good, or the perfect reality of the universe.

In its quasi-material aspect, the Light of Truth is a vibratory manifestation, with plainly visible aspects in the spiritual realms. For instance, the appearance of a "Teacher of Light" in the after-world spheres is accompanied by an illumination—beautiful and inspiring beyond description—that is as real and more real than the radiation of the sun. Persons having clairvoyant vision often are able to perceive the focused lights of teachers and angelic messengers and to feel the harmonizing warmth of the enveloping rays. Persons who are highly developed may at times have teachers or celestial helpers whose rays mingle with the electrical field or aura of the individual. Such rays tend to stimulate and exhilarate to whatever extent the individual is able to respond. By the same token, entities throwing off vibrations of a more disruptive character may find response in persons whose mental atmosphere has been colored by disharmonious thinking, and in either case the effect is amplified and magnified by the association of similar individuals in groups and communities.

Visible light, to which the eye responds, is but one wave band of a whole series of vibratory manifestations, including the oscillations of radio waves in the band of very low frequencies having long wave lengths and X-rays, gamma rays and cosmic rays in the higher frequencies with short wave lengths. The Zenor speakers have also predicted the eventual discovery of an even higher frequency of short waves from space, termed the "candic" or white ray and said to be closely associated with many of the physical processes on earth.

But these all represent only a small segment of the vibratory spectrum, and simply because we cannot measure or note by instrument a range of infinitesimally short wave lengths of incredible frequency is no proof that they do not exist. On the contrary, the teachers declare that the perceived effects, vibratory in nature, of the higher spiritual forces are of such an order, and that when these subtle rays are dominant in our environment the heavenly light is upon us. Moreover, we may speak of this effulgence as the veritable "Light of Truth," for it is to our spiritual vision the tangible evidence of peace, beauty, love and harmony and the stimulating principle of understanding.

Light also may be considered as the absence of relative darkness, the lack of disharmony or confusing interference with the basic vibratory patterns, which may be complicated and complex without being disordered. Lack of vibration would mean total, complete darkness, the total absence of creation or expression. What we experience in the struggle for adjustment to the universal vibratory patterns is more aptly described as relative darkness, a shading and obscuration of light patterns due to distortion and interference.

In the realm of psychic sight, the more orderly and harmonious vibration patterns in the higher frequency range register as light. Where distortion and disorganization occur, the psychic vision will register tones ranging from dull green, red, brown and gray to almost black, and the various psychic centers, associated with the nerve and brain centers of the body, respond and reproduce these vibrations accordingly. It is this range of light response which the discarnate entity encounters in its progress away from the earth plane, there being many octaves of color and luminosity with increasing soft brightness and supernal beauty as we advance in the higher degrees and on into the "Inner Planes" of the cosmos.

So, with the approach of the Golden Dawn, we must regard the Agashan references to it as an Age of Light as something more than a symbol. True, the assurances of leadership through wisdom and peace based on understanding have a metaphysical ring, but the new age will not be one of inactivity or the end of physical advancement. Peace will be more than an approach toward social perfection. The era of illumination will, rather, be one of inestimable growth and development, broadly founded upon vibratory harmony. So promises Agasha.

Besides a wider appreciation of what we have long called the "spiritual values" and a more general recognition of the universal nature of religion and philosophy, the material advances in the Golden Age will be stupendous. Transportation, for instance, will reach a high degree of perfection. Air travel will be completely safe, with huge ships traveling through the air at speeds above 1000 miles per hour and capable of rising and descending vertically—"like an elevator."

Similar technological progress will be made in all other fields of science and industry. For a dozen years, the Zenor teachers have been predicting a "Chemical Age" and a great "Atomic Age" in which the very foundations of our industry, as well as our society itself, will be changed. Atomic power will be available for wide use in industry, and broadcast power—which can be tuned in much like radio waves—will be widely distributed from control centers for both stationary and mobile equipment. As the Zenor forecasters put it, we will be able to "tune in" the power for our automobiles and airplanes, as well as for our homes and factories, without depending upon present relatively inefficient sources of energy.

Medical science will be completely changed, with diseases and ailments of all kinds made susceptible to treatment and cure. In many cases the diseases we have known in the past will be entirely eliminated. Understanding of the vibratory nature of physical processes will lead to the development of diagnostic and treatment devices of a highly efficient nature, completely beyond the scope of present techniques.

As an indication of the trend in this type of research, the Zenor prophets have stated that an instrument will be devised, using a type of "ray," which will enable the operator to ascertain the location of any person at a given moment merely by placing a drop of the person's blood in the machine. The device will show whether the person is at that moment on land or sea or in an airplane and will show his geographical location "down to a city block," if need be. The instrument will be constructed on the principle that the vibratory pattern of the drop of blood is the same as the basic wave pattern of the individual from which it has been taken. Therefore, the device will be able to tune in the responsive frequency of the individual, wherever he may be, making appropriate calculations as to his location. Obviously, the same principle has inestimable implications for the healing arts.

Astronomically, man will reach out into space, photographing various planets of our solar system with devices which will be sent great distances from the earth's surface. He will discover a new planet, much larger than the earth, but close to the sun and apparently revolving with the sun. It will show up on photographs of the sun and will cause a great stir among astronomers.

Eventually, man will devise methods for inter-planetary travel and will prove that some of the other planets in his system are inhabited by highly evolved beings. Meanwhile, he will continue to prove that the material universe is finite—a great atom of interrelatedness and interdependence in all its vast proportions.

Nor will the startling discoveries of exploration be confined to the heavens. Archaeologically, man will learn much of his past which will enable him to understand more about his present and future. The close of the Twentieth Century climaxes a 7000-year cycle, the high peak of which at its beginning was the Egyptian civilization described by Agasha. So far there is little evidence of that era, past Egyptian explorations having been concerned mainly with the later periods when the ideals of the enlightened time of "perfect understanding" were greatly distorted and corrupted. However, records will be found in and around the Great Pyramid to corroborate the story of this lost civilization, which lasted in its highest state for several hundred years. The tablets and records likewise will show a connection with the so-called lost Atlantean culture.

Archaeologists will also find records (some systematically stored away in cylindrical containers approximately 6000 years ago) of other rich and powerful eras of Egyptian civilization. Gold was plentiful in that land, we are told, and the structures which once were in existence and whose remains still lie beneath the sands are large and splendid beyond description. (The statement has been made through Richard Zenor that the gold of ancient Egypt, buried in the unexplored sands, would be valuable enough, according to present standards, to purchase whole countries of our modern world.)

In Siberia will be found the preserved remains of another great pre-historic civilization, portions of which were wiped out almost instantly by a wave of freezing coldness that caught families and whole cities in the midst of their activity, much in the same way that the eruption of Vesuvius trapped the population of Pompeii in 79 A.D. Buildings, homes and the bodies of their inhabitants are to be discovered, still frozen in the positions and the surroundings which they were in when the devastating cold so quickly struck. In appearance, the people will be found not unlike modern man, with a culture more modern than primitive. Huge blocks of ice will have preserved the features of some of these people almost perfectly.

Meanwhile, evidences of many forms of life long extinct will be discovered and, in some instances, revived (although there was no further explanation of this prophecy).

Explorations, too, will be made into ocean depths heretofore impossible to reach. There, scientists with appropriate apparatus will photograph buildings and other evidences of former life on now submerged continents. They will prove, in fact, that man in ages past reached a high state of technical, scientific and social development, even far beyond the advances achieved in the first part of the Twentieth Century. The huge semi-circular structures said to have been built on the "lost continent" of Atlantis will be found nearly intact and their construction studied. (The buildings were generally made of a metallic substance, having the appearance of stone but with greater strength than steel, we are told.)

In the deep valleys of the ocean bottom, other unsuspected forms of life still living and highly organized are to be found, some having a form of radiant illumination as bright as sunlight. Evidence will be brought to the surface of organisms having a remarkable social development, centering around peculiarly constructed homes on the sea floor.

Special emphasis was laid in the long-range prophecies on the philosophical and metaphysical significance of many of the discoveries, commencing generally in the years between 1948 and 1950. For instance, many new archaeological discoveries were promised in Palestine, including verifiable records of the true teachings of Jesus in their original simple form. These, it was stated, would prove that Jesus preached the laws of reincarnation and individual responsibiity, as well as the importance of spiritual communion and communication and the reality of the worlds of the after-life, with their glorified "mansions" and complex activity.

The Egyptian records, in the meantime, would supplement and corroborate the true explanations of the Christ-consciousness and link the Master Jesus with the earlier teachers of the Nile Valley.

In the realm of the spectacular, two other headline-making finds were promised: One, the golden sarcophagus of an ancient Egyptian king, with many examples of fine craftsmanship, jewelry and ornamentation, more imposing then those of Tutankhamen, and the other, first-hand descriptions of a "sleeping lama" in Tibet, land of unknown mystics, where this particular priest purports to have preserved his physical body in a trance state for hundreds of years while his spiritual body has spent most of the time in the etheric worlds.

Yet, with all of these forecasts of a brilliant and interesting future, the Zenor classes were repeatedly warned that we were in a storm we could not escape and must fortify ourselves mentally and spiritually to meet it. Of the year 1948, Agasha said:

"It is not a clear picture or a pretty picture as seen from this side. However, men are creating results now which will occur later and can be seen by us in advance, even though in the higher consciousness we do not attempt to become aware of all actions that are taking place on the earth plane."

He went on to say that a religious-economic war was already going on and would get much worse before it would get better. He spoke during the time of the frantic efforts to stop the fighting in Palestine, but he predicted that the efforts were likely to prove futile—that the fighting would spread and draw in other nations unless a miracle of compromise were performed.

He said further that "nations will rise and nations will fall"; that America itself would rise to unprecedented world leadership but would have its "falling periods," too —periods of civil dissension and near-catastrophe.

Communism, he declared, would spread, because many discouraged and disillusioned people "believe everything will be theirs without great effort." When men are finally convinced that they possess little under Communism, but are the slaves of a dictatorship without the freedoms of expression essential to a normal life, then—

"Communism will kill itself. There will be uprisings and wars, and for a number of years it will have a grip on many peoples, but finally it will die out."

Soul-less and wholly materialistic in its aims and foundations, the material advantages so glibly promised by Communism, Agasha assured us, eventually would be achieved by voluntary cooperation and understanding among men, who would recognize the all-important non-material motivations of life. With that understanding, the flood-gates of the universal supply automatically open to add the material blessings which go with applied wisdom.

Various groups advocating single but inadequate panaceas for economic ills, predicted Agasha, would give way before a general change in America without completely revolutionizing the system of free enterprise. He said (as of 1948) that the United States was in need of a great new leader, "who will work with people of high standing karmically." He prophesied that such a leader would actually arise, "almost overnight," and would work to bring about changes and establish better conditions "to provide men with all they need." The new leader would, in fact, bend his every effort toward a realization of the dream of "universal brotherhood."

Over and over, Agasha repeated:

"America is the 'New Atlantis' and will lead the world in the establishment of universal peace."

In preparation, he said, men are becoming more aware of the non-material aspects of life.

"We are now living in a psychic age, when men are inclined to seek the answers to all things."

This means, he explained, that the interest in philosophical, metaphysical and occult subjects will become more and more widespread. He also predicted that Los

Angeles would become one of the world's greatest centers for philosophical study, with thousands flocking to Southern California from all over the world. Eventually in Southern California will be erected a large structure, a "spiritual monument," on a mountain-top there—a building "strong enough to withstand earthquakes"—where occult studies will be carried on and records of the times will be deposited, much as was done in the Great Pyramid of Egypt 7000 years ago.

"A new world shall be established on this earth after 1965," Agasha prophesied, "and it will be a great peaceful age, but men shall go through the torments of hell to cleanse the earth in preparation for the change. The Golden Age is surely coming, but there are to be great shocks in the lives of men before it comes. Many strange things shall be seen, and then men shall realize the presence of the God-force within themselves and become awakened."

During the period up to 1965 will be the time when many will work for the "new dispensation," the great world-wide understanding. Between 1965 and 2020 will be the era of unrestricted advancement, the establishment of the "New Atlantis," said Agasha. After 2020 will come the "heaven on earth . . . the life God has planned for all of his children."

That does not mean, he explained, that man will be able to avoid cataclysms caused by natural forces, but he will better understand them—will control some of them and will know how to meet those he cannot control, either philosophically or scientifically. (Important climatic changes, incidentally, have also been forecast for the United States and the rest of the world.)

Further details concerning the beginning of the new

age in 1965 include this information as given by Agasha and other teachers:

Politically and economically, the world will be more perfectly organized than even the most sanguine Utopian can foresee. A world government with full delegated authority but preserving the rights of individual and group development will center in the United States, with this nation leading the world in the role of the "New Atlantis."

In this capacity, the United States will achieve both technical and social advances which will set the pattern for the rest of the world. Poverty and war will be eliminated, as well as the enslavement and repression of persons, classes and populations. Education will undergo a vital evolutionary change as educators recognize that man is living in a universal, not simply a mundane, environment which has a direct bearing on his life.

As the world organization progresses, there will be a universal language, universal citizenship, a world-wide system of monetary exchange and, most important, a universal religion, free of the petty dogmatism which has heretofore isolated and misinterpreted the truths around which churches were built.

The new language, having primarily a Latin root, will be taught throughout the world and will result, according to Agasha, in many European and other tongues taking their place with the dead languages of the past. The universal language will be simple and easily learned, but expressive, he added, and it will be the one employed by succeeding generations for thousands of years.

Economically, the world will continue to have a kind of capitalism and a banking system, but greatly changed, improved and idealized for the benefit of all.

"All will be supported properly and well supplied, without loss of individual freedom," Agasha promised. "Each will continue to earn and to keep what he earns. Individuals will take part in whatever activities they desire. All will be under one great understanding, and there will be no political competition as we now know it.

"Men shall become so close to one another that they will have to learn to adapt themselves to their world and to each other, learning to help one another and so evolve toward the Christ-consciousness right here in God's kindergarten.

"This is the generation when all these things shall come. All over the world there shall be understanding and universal brotherhood. Men shall learn and, in turn, shall beautifully express what they learn. War shall cease. Poverty shall be abolished. The prisons and charitable institutions shall be empty.

"Men shall greet each other with a loving smile, not a look of suspicion and hatred. They shall not be greedy, because there will be no reason for greed. They shall not take away from one another, because each will have all he needs.

"Man will not destroy lives, because he will love life."

And he concluded significantly:

"Atomic power shall be used to uplift mankind, not destroy it."

Previously Agasha had declared that women and young people would have a greater share in all departments of scientific and social progress. Women, he said, would not "take over power in a vulgar way, as they have sometimes done in the past because of their inexperience," but in a "beautiful, harmonious way," in keeping with a state of true equality. In the United States, he said, we could expect not one but many women presidents in future decades.

Children and the young people throughout the world would come into great power, too, many displaying unusual psychic abilities. Very young children born into this era of change and advancement will seem to grasp profound truths quickly, the reason being, said Agasha, because they have already learned in previous lives and have carried over the vestiges of their learning into this one.

The arts will progress with the sciences in the new age, and the earthly environment will be made architecturally beautiful and functionally more likable and livable in the great urban centers—the source of so much disharmony in the past.

All in all, the spirit of conflict will be replaced by the spirit of cooperation, and with this, men will reflect and reproduce the new Light of the World, devoid of the old pollutions and distortions and more appropriately in resonance with the golden light of a Heaven on Earth.

Watch for this sign, say the Teachers of Light: The very young shall begin to ask profound questions, and many of the new generation will be wise beyond their years, as well as beyond their elders, both in the science of this world and the philosophy of the universe of worlds. These wise young ones will supplant the ignorant old ones. The old ones will have become tired of the feckless stratagems of age and will be ready to yield to the messengers of the spirit. And as they lay down their burdens, the crystallization of many centuries of error, they will gladly welcome the harbingers of the new dawn, remembering that long ago it was said:

"A little child shall lead them!"

XIII

IT CAN BE SAID that we all are born with some predisposition or preconditioning toward disharmony, due to our past actions and attitudes in other lives. So we are prone to accept pain and adversity as the normal state of life on the earth and, in some instances, to regard the whole material expression as essentially sinful and evil. Neither of these concepts is true, except as we make them true by making them realities within our own individual kingdom of personal consciousness, according to Agasha.

The joyful life is neither an unattainable goal nor a sinful illusion. Pain and adversity are unnatural attributes in the ideal expressions of life, and the joy of learning through experience need not diminish the sufficiency of understanding, if the individual abstains from producing new reaction factors of a karmic nature. That does not mean he simply avoids being "bad" and does only "good," for the reaction effects are not the same for different persons. They depend upon the level of understanding; the effect of wrong thinking or action is much more drastic if it is understood to be wrong than if it is merely the result of ignorance. And the goal must always be an increase of understanding, a constant urge—without tension—toward an unfolding and realization of the mysteries of life, a never-ending search for basic answers to the eternal why of existence.

Through contemplation, meditation and reflection, unforced and unfettered, the answers can form in the objective consciousness, and the whole process, including the very process of living, can and should be joyful. It only hurts when our past and present stupidities make it hurt.

It may sometimes be difficult to apply the lessons of harmony in an environment to which we are preconditioned, but that is the test, and it is the contemplation of the meaning of the test that is important. Our souls, Agasha explains, have placed us in the environment best calculated to stimulate understanding, affording us always a choice of courses (if not always physically, then mentally), one toward the light and the other toward confusion and darkness. The shadowy vibrations of the cave of our experience often obscure and modify the true light. Yet though they lure us and deceive us, they also teach us.

Nor are we ever without help in this struggle to achieve understanding. If we want help, are willing to accept help and can help ourselves by becoming in tune with the divinely inspired sources of help and also by helping others, we will get help, not only from the flooding brilliance of universal harmony which we thus invite to ourselves but personally from the celestial messengers and the other orders of "heavenly" helpers. They are capable of focusing and transmitting the rays of cosmic power, the inspiration of divine light, to those who are ready to receive. And they are most ready to receive who have come to realize that love is the full expression of harmony, the true Christ-consciousness.

Furthermore, as we help others, we shall also be helped. Bread cast upon the water returns according to an immutable law that may be stated as a paraphrase of the Golden Rule, namely: What we do unto others shall be done to us. We earn our help and give help according to our understanding, which likewise enables us to "tune in" the help to which we are entitled. Even mere consciousness on our part of the great harmonizing light of the universal consciousness can help to disperse or at least alleviate some of the confusions which the karma of the ages has pressed in upon us.

Agasha continually emphasizes the importance of "raising our vibrations." By that he means increasing the frequency rate of our individual expressions as they are viewed in terms of vibratory patterns. And that is accomplished by raising the level of our thinking. When we raise our vibrations, we gradually cease to be in tune with the lower frequencies around us and become in rapport with the beneficent frequencies which accompany the tangible expressions of the higher spiritual orders.

Slowly, as individuals and as collections of individuals, we then begin to "tune out" the harmful potentialities of gross disharmony and "sin" (i.e., misunderstanding) and "tune in" the harmonious rays which are being constantly transmitted to us, both from the higher astral planes and the Inner Planes of what we call "outer space."

Most important of all, by this conscious process, we change our spiritual destiny and density, thus determining what frequency level of the after-life world we will gravitate to when we leave the physical body.

We are fortunate, perhaps, that Nature and the Law, the God-consciousness that is within and without us, always affords us an opportunity to select new courses which will not be complicated by the old confusions, fears, hates and prejudices of thousands of years of objective memory. The memory is there, but it is the ineffaceable memory of the soul. The soul, being a part of the God-consciousness, perfectly evaluates from life to life the requirements of the ego for perfect individualization through self-expression and self-realization. The evolving, unfolding ego is guided into those situations which will afford the best chance for conscious self-development and self-understanding through the exercise of the power of reflection and choice and through the payment of karmic debts. Then, in time, when we are self-consciously in a position to evaluate our memory in terms of the universal consciousness, that which is relevant or ready to be absorbed into the total meaning of experience will be recalled, Agasha teaches. Nothing is ever lost; every act is registered, and every thought, word and attitude is also an action which produces reaction. Dissonance replaces harmony only when we choose to strike the wrong chords by our responses. We are privileged, teaches Agasha, to discover for ourselves the combinations which are resonant and harmonious. In that way we ultimately discover ourselves.

According to the Agashan explanations, we remain oblivious of much of the past until we are able to absorb into our consciousness and our conscience the significance of the lesson to be learned from a particular experience or series of experiences. Complete and unalterable records of all experiences are stored in the memory of the soul. In addition, they make their permanent impressions upon the etheric atmosphere of the earth, establishing the "causes" which mature into later results.

Complete memory of past lives would cloud the judgment and unduly warp the evaluation of current experiences. When we are ready and equipped with sufficient spiritual power, we will remember and evaluate. The soul in each life, searching for the perfect individual expression, gives itself an opportunity to reflect new images and thus provides a way for the consciousness to reflect upon them, without being weighted down by all of the accumulated errors and prejudices of the past.

Even if we cannot change our physical destiny (in some cases, because of the submerged memory which is the storehouse of our karma), we can command or change our consciousness and our reflections upon our destiny, which at the moment is whatever is happening to us. By contemplating the meaning of our current experiences, we become free to evaluate all experience. So do we "learn our lessons" and advance accordingly. By enhancing our understanding, we are also in a position to change some of the events of our destiny or transmute the effects upon our consciousness. As a man thinks, so is he. Therefore, we may weigh our destiny by this axiom:

It is human to err but to profit by one's errors is the divine road to freedom and enlightenment.

Eventually we achieve the blessed catharsis of realization and understanding, either through pain and suffering or by the more pleasant method of acquiring wisdom through conscious self-development and consideration of the teachings and expressions of wisdom brought forth by others. Or it may be a combination of both. In the past, the ancient mystery schools were established to provide initiation into the fraternity of understanding by means of a program of unfoldment, rather than by trial and error. The world is now going through what the teachers call the "process of elimination," in order that its inhabitants may freely choose to adopt a program of wise understanding, rather than trial and error.

None of us may delegate our search for understanding to a preacher, priest or director without compromising our freedom and the efficacy of our unfoldment. We may never rest comfortably in the assurance that we have a free pass to the heavenly consciousness because we have subscribed to the rituals of outside agencies, says Agasha. The directive force must finally come from within ourselves, if we would be successful in our quest for illumination. Yet many avenues of initiation are open to us. We are warned merely not to confuse the forms with the substance of our unfoldment. When we recognize the significance of the forms and that they include all of our expressions, our choosing to live in harmony with universal law becomes almost automatic. All of our expressions are a real part of our experience and of the rites of initiation, though they be but the shadowforms projected from our real selves. This is the unreal reality of our existence and the insubstantial substance of our learning.

No neophyte in his training for the initiation can be wholly without error, no matter how wisely he directs the heavenly quest. We have made an error when we make a mistake in one or more of our expressions, but it is the heavenly dispensation, the soul-administered law of evolution, that we shall have unlimited opportunities to correct the error. We may correct it only by understanding the forces our error has set in motion, so that the "sin" is expiated either by new trials designed to bring home the lesson or by an inspired recognition of the meaning of the Law without the painful discipline of new trials.

For most of us, our existence is one long series of errors. As we project our expressions amoeba-like into the fluid of our environment, we are punished—or, rather, we punish ourselves—most severely for deliberate and knowing violations of the natural laws. At first, we are given the gentle push to keep us on the path; then, if we fail, the more violent shove—by the God-self which is seeking the perfect expression through us.

The purpose of life is to find the perfect expression of our true selves—an eons-long process, no portion of which is unimportant or in any way to be despised. So to discover the purpose of life we must ever search for its meaning, by molding and observing the imperfection of our currently inadequate expressions.

There is an interesting term used by the Agashan teachers which symbolizes the power of free will and free development within the limits of accumulated karma. They often refer to personalities manifesting through Richard Zenor as "forces," or when used as an inclusive term, as "the forces." Such a "force" represents an individualized center of consciousness, whether encased in a physical body or not. These vortices or conditioned centers of consciousness and energy are as much a part of the whole as the rippling waves upon a pond. The word "force" well describes them, for they are individualized manifestations of the total force which supports the universe. It is the force that urges self-development and underlies the advancement, stimulation and inspiration of the less developed by powerful, advanced personalized "forces." These manifest by means of their own focused wave motions and through their transmission of Divine Light, into which they boundlessly extend.

No mechanical analogy can ever adequately represent the spiritual verities. However, if we understand ourselves as focal points or "forces" in the great multi-dimensional sea of ordered consciousness, producing our own expressions as vehicles of experience, even though they be but imperfect illusions of our true state, we may touch the button of realization which goes beyond all words and analogies and floods us with divine illumination. Each of us is a force for good and beauty, if we choose, and as we so choose, we transmute the lessons of the past into joyful living and learning for the future. Those who are leaders become the expressions and the "forces" through which the combined experience of peoples and nations are blended into related lessons. For we are all related within the Law, says Agasha, all participants in classroom activities that make each of us responsible and responsive to the other class members, as well as to the expressions which we unfold from ourselves.

Some have achieved great forcefulness by isolating themselves from the disturbing centers of disruptive force. They are ascetics, adepts and illumined ones who have achieved by themselves a high degree of consciousness, and the force of their isolated centers of understanding sends forth light to the rest of the world. However, those who achieve a measure of illumination in the midst of everyday distractions become towers of light and strength beyond praise. In the end, it will be our ability to absorb and reflect the heavenly light while leading what we call normal lives that will prepare us for the Golden Age, Agasha teaches. That is why he prescribes no special rituals, no violent departures from normal living, in the common sense training of his students. By being ever conscious of the divine harmony and by giving recognition in our thoughts to the help of celestial messengers, we further expand the areas of peace, happiness and concord around us.

And as we give recognition, we open wider the channels within ourselves for additional help, power, inspiration and understanding, easing the reactions to past misunderstanding and cushioning the shocks of our karma.

At times the inadequate statements of the principles of the universe—which are little understood by any man, else he would not be here—seem difficult to apply to the problems of practical living, but it comes down to a full application of the same basic virtues which have been taught by the great teachers of all ages and which man has found to be practical, even for his own selfish good. Now we begin to understand why virtues are necessary to life. Virtues, Christian virtues, if you please, are practical and scientific because their expression is directly linked to the wave motions, the harmonizing vibrations of our individual "force." Each of us is a transmitter, as well as a receiver, of vibratory power. The thought-force which is generated by kindliness, cooperation, love, helpfulness, tolerance, patience, charity of thought and action, by friendliness, benevolence, generosity of spirit and substance, good will and integrity in all of its meanings, has more than abstract importance.

These are values which produce and reproduce spiritual light, manifested by a regularity, rather than a confusion, of wave patterns, regardless of their complexity. And they reflect back upon their originator, as well as the receiver. Where a selfish, hurtful purpose is expressed by the individual—either hurtful to himself or others—the mental atmosphere is disturbed and the psychic atmosphere of the world is further disordered proportionately. Life is degraded, and the perfect light of spirituality, the myriad vibration patterns of blessed harmony and the source-forces of beautiful living are shut out.

The positive manifestations of harmonious living likewise include all the arts and sciences which tend to produce symmetry in our design for living. Squalor and ugliness are expressions of disharmony. Orderliness and physical beauty are expressions of concord and in themselves tend to stimulate harmonious responses within the individual, contributing positively to his health and well-being, as well as to that of the social group.

Ill-health, unhappiness and mental suffering are due to the tensions which we have inherited from our unlearned lessons of the past and which we prolong in the present. Such tensions and imbalance inhibit the harmonizing effect of the universal light, just as eye strain—tension, imbalance—inhibits and distorts the images of visible light. Though the discordant condition may be only local from a universal point of view, the local clouding of the general light-harmony persists until the lessons of resonance and reaction applicable to each special case are learned.

There is no question now as to the evidence that every person is both a broadcaster and a receiver of wave patterns which help to make or complicate his environment. Therefore, as he grows into the light, he becomes as a light unto himself and to others. Agasha's principal purpose in speaking through the telephone-like mediumship of Richard Zenor has been, as he has often said, to multiply the numbers of those who are able to receive and transmit the light—in its literal form and as a symbol of true understanding. The masters of hatred and the creatures of fear, who for so long have broadcast disruptive wave motions that have darkened and polluted the sensitive vibratory atmosphere of the earth, must inevitably succumb to the superior pressure of universal orderliness, the perfect expression which we call Divine Love and which we are privileged to individualize as expressions of the Christ-consciousness.

On the earth level, this becomes the compassionate love of each for the other, no matter how degraded or hateful be the other's station; in the higher realms, it becomes the love of universal truth and perfect understanding, extending to all expressions and the whole of creation as aspects of evolving consciousness. Just as the child adores each of his toy soldiers in the playroom's warring armies, so does the universal soul feel compassion for the struggling, learning, striving souls of the yet unlearned.

We have as the final promise for the "bright future" a pledge that man, at last, is approaching the great spiritual awakening of which he has always been inherently capable, an awakening born of a climactic cataclysm of pain but giving hope of a world-wide appreciation of the completely practical aspects of harmonious living. The illusions of matter and the delusions of its misuse will have become incidents in the lesson plan of the universe, no longer important in themselves and no longer the prime objectives in a restricted range of consciousness. We will have sought and found the Kingdom of Heaven within ourselves, and all the rest will be added unto us; for our illusory images, the valued stuff of our lessons and experience, will take orderly shape in the reflected glory of the One that is All and the beautiful and good that is the divine expression of the One.

We learn, therefore, that the purpose of life is to discover the meaning of life, and while each life, through its individual expressions, has its own meaning, all meanings lead finally to the Infinite Source of all that is purpose in life, the Divine Consciousness we call God.

XIV

H EAR, NOW, the words of Agasha, humble in their simplicity, eternal in their verity. Gleaned as fragments from many reapings, they represent but a token of the total harvest. May they be implanted as seeds of wisdom in the hearts of men and grow and multiply with abundance in the vineyard of the Lord.

These, then, are the words, to be sown and grown by each within himself, according to his own understanding:

Be patient with yourself and the world that is around you, for the earth is young in experience, and the cycles of its development are far from complete.

* * *

Fear not, for fear begets the thing most feared. Be ever cheerful. Try to live each day of your life in a beautiful way, enjoying everything about you or adjusting yourself within your own consciousness to that which you feel cannot be enjoyed. You are here to enjoy your "good karma" and to learn your lessons from all that your soul has brought within the reach of your kingdom, and your "kingdom" is all that comes within the range of your consciousness.

* * *

God will see you through, the God-self within you. When you have found yourself, you have found God, the universal principle.

* * *

There is much to confuse us on this earth plane, but it is within our own individual consciousness that we are free to learn and to grow. You are the master of your own individual kingdom, your own conscious self, and no one can invade that kingdom without your permission.

* * *

Do not be caught in the sea of evil and contention. Contemplate, rather, the working of the law of cause and effect within yourself and in all that is around you. Seek ever to alleviate the force of evil with the harmonious force of good.

* * *

As we evolve and learn and grow, we become shining lights to assist ourselves and to guide others. Be ever conscious of the light and of life and of the privilege of having experiences which unfold the light.

* * *

We must seek within the God-kingdom that dwells within ourselves. We must take inventory of ourselves, of the deeds and thoughts which tend to hold us to this earth consciousness. We must become calm and peaceful within ourselves, recognizing that which is holding us back and that which we are to overcome through understanding, in order that we may grow into the light which is a manifestation of our true selves.

*　　*　　*

Be still and know that "I am with you"; that is, the God-part of yourself. You are a part of all there is, complete within yourself, as an expression of the universal consciousness.

*　　*　　*

When you are ready, the master will appear—the "master" that is within you—but as you become ready, we also can appear to help you on your way.

*　　*　　*

Amid the confusions of the world, know within yourself that "I am the way, and I am the light," the true self that is the God-self. Live each day for the spirit. Send forth noble thoughts to inspire each man within his own kingdom and attract to yourself the blessed light sent forth by the Teachers of Light.

*　　*　　*

"I am the way; I am the light"—and the "I am" is yourself, the spark of divinity that is your true self.

*　　*　　*

God gives no man any gift that he himself has not earned.

*　　*　　*

We must go through certain conditions to learn our lessons and to learn to adjust ourselves to the laws of life. We go through these experiences in order that we may become individualized in the consciousness of God, but the real life is not here. It is yet to come.

*　　*　　*

Every life is a life of new opportunity. Therefore, it is a beautiful life to the degree that we take advantage of our opportunity.

*　　*　　*

It is a privilege for us to have our experiences on this earth plane, and we do not expect to become perfect within a single lifetime. But we expect to learn our lessons from day to day, so that we will not need to repeat each lesson continually in the great school of experience.

*　　*　　*

Each of you has a cross to bear, but your cross shall become lighter as you learn, grow and expand your consciousness in the Light of the Universe and become attuned to the Infinite Consciousness.

*　　*　　*

No matter how loudly we cry out, that alone will not help us. The more we murmur and rebel, the more we will have to work out. The sooner we are quiet and peaceful within ourselves, the sooner we will find the solution to our problems.

*　　*　　*

If we continue to complain about our circumstances, we hold ourselves back spiritually and attract to ourselves new circumstances which will bring home to us the lesson we have to learn. We must realize that we are growing and expressing that which is necessary to strengthen ourselves and increase our awareness.

* * *

Be grateful for each experience and welcome it as an opportunity to learn a lesson. Say to yourself, "No matter how difficult it is, I will learn it, and I will benefit from it." Say to yourself, "I am part of the universe. I am complete unto the universal consciousness, God. I am grateful to God who has given me the opportunity to learn my lessons and to learn the purpose of life. I bless everything I receive. I live fully each day. 'I am the way; I am the light.' I am complete within myself, within my own kingdom, which is an expression of the complete universal consciousness."

* * *

Each tear you shed represents an experience that will turn into a pearl of wisdom as you accept its lesson.

* * *

The soul determines your tests according to your karma and your spiritual awakening.

* * *

We are here to attain the soul consciousness, which in reality is the God-consciousness, and it is our soul which puts us through the tests that lead to our unfoldment and strengthen our understanding.

* * *

Some of our material trials seem harsh, but all are brought to us for a purpose.

* * *

We often go through tests to shake off the mental bodies which tend to disturb us.

* * *

We may make the same mistakes over and over, but as we do, we build up the negative mental bodies in our aura which result in our having more to overcome.

* * *

The burdens of the material world are lifted as the lessons of the spiritual universe are learned.

* * *

We earn everything we receive in this life. We earn every step of the way.

* * *

As the wheel of life turns, our tests become more severe in the absence of understanding, but as we learn, our tests become welcome and joyful experiences.

* * *

I do not make the law. I only come to tell you what the law means to you.

* * *

The Teachers of Light pass judgment on no man, for the soul determines in each his own destiny according to his spiritual awakening.

* * *

I do not set myself beyond any individual. We are all one with the universal consciousness. I do not judge any person. Each is his own judge and his own best teacher.

* * *

It is God's will that we all will to understand God.

* * *

Sin is a lack of understanding, growing out of that which hurts ourselves and our fellow man. By our sins— our mistakes of understanding—we accumulate debts which we must eventually pay. All of our books must finally be balanced to inherit our kingdom in "heaven."

* * *

God has put us on the earth to learn our lessons individually. We are our own best teachers.

* * *

Wisdom is not hidden within. It *is* within. We need only to open the door of the soul to release it.

* * *

As we arouse the soul, all can be revealed in a most blessed way.

* * *

Only when the soul is awakened can we understand what is given in the higher light.

* * *

We are seeking soul illumination, so that all of our outward expressions shall be as perfect as our true selves. But illumination must come from within.

* * *

We become absorbed in the universal light, the perfect state, not merely by wishing and praying but by earning, learning and living.

* * *

In reality, all that is true has been given to you before. All that you are now doing is to open the door so that the wisdom within can come forth. In so many lives we have done so much to close the door to wisdom—to information and reformation. Now we are attempting to awaken the soul, so that it can take full command.

* * *

All shall eventually reach an understanding of the laws of life and the reason for their being here. Through the cycles of their experiences in relation to other souls who are repeatedly in the same classrooms with them, each of them will finally learn.

* * *

Ours is a practical philosophy, with no special rules or rituals except the ritual of living harmoniously and naturally, having our experiences and developing the beauty of our expressions until we and all about us are in tune with the Infinite Consciousness, the Divine Light.

* * *

If we depend upon rituals, rites and incantations for

our advancement, that is a violation of the law. The spiritual life must be learned and earned.

*   *   *

God is not one individual but all individuals.

*   *   *

God is expressing Himself through every form of life, on the earth and in the etheric realms as well.

*   *   *

We are all gradually evolving back to the Great Source, the Great Motivator of all things, but individualized within the God-consciousness, which supplies the generative power for the universe.

*   *   *

As we descend into the physical world, we are the "fallen angels" who have taken on the lower frequencies of gross matter to perfect our individual awareness of the meaning of the heavenly home, to which we will some day return.

*   *   *

You are becoming individualized, as God so deemed it. We are all evolving back to the Core of Life to take our places with those arisen ones we call the Pillars of Light, the gods of the universe.

*   *   *

We are all perfect in reality. We are simply striving through our unfoldment to bring that perfection into the light. We are all God's children, and we all have the same opportunity to express our perfection.

*   *   *

No soul is damned for all eternity, and no soul is ever damned temporarily except by the imperfections of its consciousness.

*   *   *

You are not preparing for eternity; you are living in eternity now. You are not preparing for the spirit; you are a spirit now.

*   *   *

Eternity is not a future state. You are living in eternity as much as you ever will be.

*   *   *

You are a spirit as surely as any other spirit. The only difference is that you are still encased in a physical shell, which is your earthly home and the temple of your initiation into a higher consciousness.

*   *   *

You are as much a spirit now as you ever will be, although you are encased in a physical body, and I on this side am not. We are both spirits, working on different frequencies and manifesting on different planes or in different degrees of consciousness.

*   *   *

When you leave this earth, all that you have accumulated materially remains with the earth and cannot be taken with you. All that you have learned can be taken with you.

* * *

It is only what we have earned spiritually that we can take with us when we come to this side of life. All else goes back to the earth as dust, rust and ashes.

* * *

The spiritual life is the real life, and the material life is the unreal. You do not begin to live really until you die and leave behind the delusions of matter, for death is not a disaster. It is a graduation.

* * *

Birth is far more mysterious than death. Death is easy, but birth is far more difficult and intricate.

* * *

You are a miniature universe within yourself. You represent all there is.

* * *

Each atom is a world within itself.

* * *

Remember, before the worlds were born, you were, and after they cease to exist, you will continue to be.

* * *

Your body alone does not represent you. It is but a vehicle for you to employ as an expression of yourself. It is not you.

*   *   *

Since your body is your vehicle of expression, guard it well and use it well.

*   *   *

You live with yourself, and the sum total of yourself is what you are and what you represent yourself to be. You are today all that you have been in all of your lives, and you will be tomorrow what you make of your lessons and opportunities today.

*   *   *

Become calm and peaceful within yourself so that you and your bodily vehicle will work in tune with the universe. When you become quiescent, you are able to attract to yourself the teachers' rays, and these become a living reality in order for you, in turn, to become a positive, happy individual.

*   *   *

The vehicle (body) through which you are expressing yourself at the moment must be cared for and preserved in the best way possible, in order to make the best of your opportunities and so that it will provide a clear channel for the higher forces which can manifest through it.

*   *   *

The sum total of the many lives you have lived is the result which you are today.

*   *   *

The force of destiny is not outside of us; it is within us

* * *

We attract experiences and make our destiny according to our karmic thinking.

* * *

We are attracted to certain conditions in life by the law of attraction and the law of compensation, which we call karma and destiny. It is how we meet these conditions that constitutes the test.

* * *

It is possible to peer into the future and to see what the results shall be even thousands of years from now, based upon what is being created by our thoughts and actions in the etheric realms today.

* * *

We work out our old karma and avoid making new karma by cleansing our consciousness of the hates, fears, antagonisms, irritations, animosities and tensions which close the door to information and reformation.

* * *

Everything is recorded in the soul. Our soul puts us through tests according to our understanding and to increase our understanding. You are here to attain the perfect soul consciousness, not merely to maintain the body, but the body is the blessed vehicle for the developing expressions of the soul.

* * *

Learning the principles of life is important, but applying what you have learned of the principles in your everyday life is more important, for only in that way can you be sure you have learned.

*   *   *

Jesus was trying to be a living example of what he taught. He taught men to love one another, but he also taught that men would make many mistakes and that God would not condemn them but would give them another opportunity to learn.

*   *   *

Try ever to recognize the good that is within all things and within yourself and your fellow man.

*   *   *

The only way you can have brotherly love on earth is to have brotherly love in your heart—by understanding the purpose of life and where you are going when you leave this physical life.

*   *   *

We must go through the process of elimination before peace can be established.

*   *   *

In your present cycle, you are collectively going through the cleansing process, the process of elimination, in preparation for the new cycle, which is to start in 1965.

*   *   *

The world is going through a time of great crisis, but

this is also a period of cleansing—the time when the way will be prepared for the white forces, the Teachers of Light, whose universal "religion" will one day prevail among mankind.

*   *   *

Many of you will not reach the period after 1965 when peace will be established on earth, but you will be able to assist and observe from the spiritual realms. You are now going through one of the most trying periods the world has ever known, and millions will have their trials and tribulations. Live your life fully and normally from day to day and know that God—the Christ-self within you—will protect you according to the light of your understanding.

*   *   *

Our philosophy helps us to eliminate fear of the future. While all about us is confusion and turmoil, we do not become oblivious or isolate ourselves from this evil to escape its evil effects but cleanse and fortify ourselves spiritually, so that we may become channels for the great power that can come to us from the reservoir of good in the higher planes. In this way we help ourselves, and we help others. Nothing can destroy us but ourselves.

*   *   *

In the coming age of enlightenment, each will live according to his learning and his desires. Each in his own category according to his advancement will come to understand the purpose of life and where he is going when he leaves the earth life.

*   *   *

It is up to ourselves to protect ourselves and to fortify ourselves against the inferior vibrations of undeveloped men and their environments.

*   *   *

Where there is life, there is the supply, if we but expand our consciousness to receive it. Seek the kingdom of heaven within and, as Master Jesus taught, all else shall be added unto you.

*   *   *

It is your attitude toward material things that is important, not their cost. You are here to enjoy life and the things which God has placed here for your learning and enjoyment. You are to be grateful to God, the universal principle, that you have been permitted to remain in the physical body to learn your lessons and perfect your expressions.

*   *   *

We do not despise material things, but through our unfoldment we are earning that which is much more substantial in spirit.

*   *   *

As you give out power to your fellow man, you shall receive power. As you take power, you shall lose yourself. As you give out, so shall you receive. As you fill your neighbor's cup, so shall yours be filled.

*   *   *

There are always men who seek to lead other men into slavery. But it is they who become slaves to the things of this world and separated from the bountiful heritage which is the spiritual light of all the worlds.

* * *

Intelligence and intellect relate to things that are learned (and our learning is important), but wisdom comes from the breath of God over a long period of time, as we earn it and refine our learning from life to life.

* * *

It is a thinking individual who becomes able quietly and peacefully to search within himself. He is a strong man, indeed, who can think for himself, and he who thinks for himself is a free man, indeed.

* * *

It is a strong man, too, who will stand for what is good; who will become humble and peaceful, saying, "I am ready for my test and will not rebel." This is truly a strong man.

* * *

Humility is one of the hardest lessons for man to learn. Many in occult work seem to be as stubborn as those with little understanding. The higher we progress and the more we unfold, the humbler we become. Many times occultists allow the ego to inflate and feel they are so high in their unfoldment they have no great problems to overcome. If that were true, they would not be in the body, and the errors of their thinking will bring them greater problems as they go along.

*   *   *

The wise man is ever humble and preserves a willingness to be humble in the eyes of the great or the small. The farther we advance the humbler we become.

*   *   *

If we see only the worst side of life, magnifying the confusions and distortions of life about us, we reflect these things within our own kingdom and so become a part of them. We have the right to place whatever we wish within the kingdom of our consciousness, for in reality each of us can say:

"I am master of myself, I am all powerful, and nothing can come to me of an inferior nature. I am peace; I am power; I am all there is—I am complete within myself [the infinitely intelligent and inseparable recapitulation of the universe]."

*   *   *

Know, then, blessed children, that there is peace within your soul, and the world shall have peace when you have learned, when you have grown and when you have known the truth that is within your soul.

*   *   *

Be prepared; be receptive; be attuned.

THE AUTHOR

James Crenshaw
(1908–1994)

JAMES CRENSHAW was a Los Angeles newspaper reporter and writer of more than 25 years' experience. He had his share of the rough-and-tumble life that goes with covering all the many-sided happenings of the day's news.

Crenshaw was a member of the staffs of daily newspapers in Los Angeles and San Diego, and was a specialist in court cases that make news. Thus he dveloped a keen respect for the "rules of evidence" and applied the legal method of taking and weighing evidence to a great extent in gathering his facts for *Telephone Between Worlds.*

With a rich background as a trained observer, Mr. Crenshaw began in 1935 to collect material on the "who, what, when, where and why" of the after-life world through the instrumentality of Richard Zenor (1911–1978). He considered this material to be part of the biggest story of our age — solid proof of the existence of another world, with logical, reasonable explanations of what it is like and what it means to us here.

Born in Richland, Oregon, in 1908, Mr. Crenshaw moved to San Diego at an early age. He graduated from the University of California in 1929. His writings include numerous articles on psychic subjects.